A COUNSELLOR'S COMPANION

CREATIVE ADVENTURES FOR CHILD COUNSELLORS, PARENTS AND TEACHERS

KIM BILLINGTON
M. Couns. M. Narrative Therapy. B.Ed

Illustrated by Tamar Dolev BFA

First published by Ultimate World Publishing 2021
Copyright © 2021 Kim Billington

ISBN

Paperback: 978-1-922497-66-6
Ebook: 978-1-922497-67-3

Kim Billington has asserted her rights under the Copyright, Designs and Patents Act 1988 to be identified as the author of this work. The information in this book is based on the author's experiences and opinions. The publisher specifically disclaims responsibility for any adverse consequences which may result from use of the information contained herein. Permission to use information has been sought by the author. Any breaches will be rectified in further editions of the book.

All rights reserved. No part of this publication may be reproduced, stored in or introduced into a retrieval system, or transmitted in any form, or by any means (electronic, mechanical, photocopying, recording or otherwise) without the prior written permission of the author. Any person who does any unauthorised act in relation to this publication may be liable to criminal prosecution and civil claims for damages. Enquiries should be made through the publisher.

Cover design: Ultimate World Publishing
Layout and typesetting: Ultimate World Publishing
Editor: Marinda Wilkinson
Cover image and illustrations: Tamar Dolev

Ultimate World Publishing
Diamond Creek,
Victoria Australia 3089
www.writeabook.com.au

Testimonials

Kim has a unique ability in getting to the core of an issue. With her extensive knowledge and practical skills, she can transform lives with one small story or insightful intervention. She is a born teacher, who always finds a way to explain a concept or impart an idea that is both easily understood, and helpful in bringing about positive change.

Sue Nielsen – Psychologist
BA Psychology (Hons)

Kim is an experienced narrative therapist and dynamic presenter. She is highly skilled in taking a complex theory and bringing it to life with clarity, passion, relevant clinical examples and relatable experiences. Participants in Kim's training workshops love her personal approach and come away with knowledge and immediately useable skills.

Jacki Short –
Clinical Director of Sydney Centre for Creative Change
Registered Counselling Psychologist and
Play Therapist

I had the privilege of having Kim as my supervisor and peer group facilitator. She is an encouraging and supportive mentor, expanding my thinking and providing space to explore creative ways of counselling. Kim's passion for her work is inspiring and she never fails to be totally present in each of our sessions.

Nothara Suraweera – School Counsellor
BA; M. Couns

Sessions with Kim helped my son find the words (and pictures) to express his fears and sorrow, and then to process the pain. It was a big relief for us all to realise we'd be okay.

DJ – Mother of 7-year-old

Kim has a unique talent that enables her to combine her creative and expressive skills to work with children and safely support them to tell their life stories. Her knowledge and wisdom make this an essential guide for all counsellors and therapists engaging with children.

Susan Konstantas – Bereavement Counsellor
BA Disability Studies; GradDip Coaching & Counselling; ACA-L2

I am grateful for Kim's skillful and gentle supervision guidance that has evoked my own feeling of hope as I progress in my counselling role. One of the therapeutic activities that I commonly use in my practice is based on Kim's creative way of introducing animal images to assist children understand fight/flight/freeze responses. Kim's expertise in family violence has shaped my work with families, with a particular emphasis on the strength-based approach.

**Dajana Sprajcer-Simeunovic –
Family Violence Counsellor
M. Couns; GradDip Couns; Dip AppSci**

As a family mediator, I value Kim's skills to engage with children prior to Child Informed Mediation, and consult with them through her therapeutic interventions, to bring their voices to the mediation process. Her ways of giving feedback, even to reluctant parents, enables them to see the impact of family separation on their children, and become more child-centred. Kim's energy and ability to make children of any age feel comfortable and connected is a gift of hers.

**Michelle Zelig – Nationally Accredited Mediator
Family Dispute Resolution Practitioner**

Kim's suggestions for practice are accessible, engaging and reflect her deep understanding and rich counselling experience. I can always rely on her for thoughtful and creative ways to work with clients.

**Kate Whelen – Carer Counsellor
GradDip Couns & Psychotherapy**

Kim is insightful and knows the right questions to ask. She creatively adapts play experiences to support children and youth to tell and process their stories. I have greatly valued her voice in my professional journey, and continue to look to her for guidance.

**Suzy Costello – Counsellor SocS(Psych),
GradDip Psych, GradDip Ed(ECE), M. Couns**

Having worked with Kim over a number of years I am impressed by her wide counselling experience leading to respect for the inner capacity of children. Her book is based in recognised research and celebrates her creative focus on attunement, using fun, play, curiosity and exploration of story. The value in this work will be seen in the generation of greater understanding for parents and carers as they meet the challenges of fostering wellbeing for children. I am very pleased to endorse this new publication.

**Dr Vivienne Mountain
Supervisor – University of Divinity**

Dedication

From author, Kim Billington:

To my children, Claire, Peter and Charli Rose,
and grandson, Sterling
who continue to share me with others.
Thank you. You fill my heart to overflowing.

From artist, Tamar Dolev:

I dedicate this book to my parents for their unconditional love, support and belief. To my aunt, my brother, sister-in-law, and beautiful nieces Liv and Mia for their love and creativity. My fur child Billie for her endless cuddles and adventures. Her legacy will live on amongst the pages.

Contents

Testimonials	iii
Dedication	vii
Foreword: Welcome to Counselling	xi
Introduction: Counselling Superpowers	xiii
Chapter 1: Colossal Courage	1
Chapter 2: What's Wonderful About You?	21
Chapter 3: Introduce Me to the Problem	37
Chapter 4: Hacking the Problem	59
Chapter 5: Roller-Coaster of Emotions	77
Chapter 6: The Fork in the Road	97
Chapter 7: The Unfairness of Loss	117
Chapter 8: Therapeutic Stories	139
Chapter 9: Power Rules	155
Chapter 10: Philosophy – Making Sense of Life's Problems	175

Chapter 11: Who's on Your Team?	189
Chapter 12: Saying Goodbye	205
Appendix 1: Safety First	217
Appendix 2: Summary of Narrative Therapy	225
References	227
About the Author	233
About the Illustrator	237
Acknowledgements	239
Testimonials	241
Offers	245
Speaker Bio	247

Foreword:
Welcome to Counselling
(Written to a child who is starting counselling)

Starting counselling? Welcome! Counselling helps people with all sorts of problems: small, medium or BIG ones. So, strap on your seatbelt, because counselling is an adventure!

Counselling can be a good place to talk about tricky problems. Problems usually come uninvited. How unfair is that!

Every adult was once a small child, and we know that problems can be annoying and make it hard to have fun.

Parents might call a counsellor when they're not sure what to do next. You might come to your first meeting along with your parent, on a screen, or in person at a counselling room.

Counselling is your special time. It's a safe space, free from shame or blame. There will be no finger-pointing at you. Because we stand together and point the finger at The Problem. We put The Problem under the spotlight.

Sometimes you get to talk, draw and play. Your counsellor will also want to hear about your proud moments, friendships, interests and your ideas about dealing with The Problem.

Like wearing a new pair of shoes, at first counselling can feel a bit awkward, but it will soon feel okay.

Life is a journey, and every now and then problems come along. So, put on those new shoes. Choosing counselling is saying 'Yes!' to a new direction.

There was an ancient Chinese man called Lao Tzu. He was very wise and said:

'The 1,000-mile journey begins with the first step'.

Introduction: Counselling Superpowers

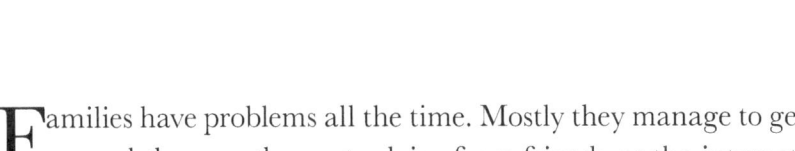

Families have problems all the time. Mostly they manage to get around them or they get advice from friends or the internet. Some get stuck with what to do next.

Counselling is a safe space and provides a dedicated time to address difficulties. Child counsellors have a fount of fabulous, fun activities and therapeutic approaches that can help children talk about and work through tricky problems, and facilitate change.

Children may be struggling with reduced motivation, stress, frustration and finding it hard to relax. They may be surviving refugee trauma, family violence, abuse, divorce, out-of-home care, and other losses where feelings of powerlessness, sadness and anger become regular, unwelcome guests.

How this book can help

The suggestions in this book can be used in both in-person and online counselling, and may be adapted to suit different ages: children (4–12 years) and young people (13–18 years). Some are my original, creative ideas that have been effective and well received by children, while others such as Externalising The Problem (Chapter 3), The Hero's Journey (Chapter 8) and Tree of Life (Chapter 11) have been gathered from various sources over the years.

In the foreword, I shared a letter I give to children new to counselling. Children want and need information about how they might be expected to participate, and about the limits of confidentiality (outlined in Appendix 1).

Throughout this book, parents, teachers and children will discover accessible keys to unlocking ways to deal with annoying problems. In Chapter 3, techniques such as finding a name for The Problem, and measuring the size of The Problem are introduced. Chapter 9 is devoted to noticing how there are power dynamics at play in every problem, and every encounter. Who we are and what we believe affects how we are in the presence of children and their families, and Chapter 10 brings to our attention the helpfulness of knowing what we, as counsellors hold to be true or important in life.

The activities described use imaginative, creative expressive arts and existential musings—and all are woven with serious fun, to enhance self-understanding and facilitate change.

Many chapters include therapeutic stories, rich with ancient wisdoms. These are powerful with clients of all ages who are struggling to make sense of their journey. Such folktales were a natural part of cultures in times gone by, and are becoming more widely used once more. They offer people hope as they search for ways to get through hard times, and Chapter 8 includes more background about their use.

Open the book anywhere, and you will find a smorgasbord of counselling approaches and doorways to new possibilities.

Why I wrote the book

Inspired by narrative therapy's founders, Michael White and David Epston, I have been developing the art of asking quirky questions, woven with metaphors for years. This adventurous style of counselling seems to stimulate new perspectives and ideas, that can make The Problem look quite different and not as daunting. A summary of the key aspects of narrative practice is found in Appendix 2.

After years of practising, researching and developing exciting techniques that children and young people find helpful and fun, I began to teach these to other professionals and had several articles published in the *Counselling Australia Journal*.

I received encouraging feedback from counsellors, parents, teachers and social workers about the efficacy of these approaches, and have been asked countless times to write a book.

I seized the opportunity of the seemingly never-ending COVID-19 lockdown in Melbourne, recruited my artist friend, Tamar Dolev to bring her talents to these pages, and so began another new beginning.

I have found that since 'The Big Pause' of COVID-19, many children are feeling quite comfortable meeting their counsellor remotely. Online therapy can be exciting and convenient, and might suit many 21st century, tech-savvy children. We now all have a chance to explore different ways children can express their concerns and find safe connections.

Working with parents

In supervision with counsellors who are transitioning to working with children, two questions regularly come up: 'How should we communicate with parents?' and 'How do we meet the demands of parents?' Some parents are worried their child won't agree to counselling. These questions and concerns are considered throughout the book, and you will find some interesting ideas about ways to respond in Chapter 1.

For parents, the decision to engage a counsellor is often difficult. What courage it takes to put your family's private matters in the hands of a stranger. You might have a single session with the whole family, and brainstorm to come up with ideas, or you may recommend parents look up professional accredited bodies such as the Psychotherapy and Counselling Federation of Australia (PACFA) or Australian Counselling Association (ACA) to find a suitable counsellor.

If you feel a child is especially unwell in their mental health, you can call Kids Helpline on 1800 55 1800, and have a conversation/consultation with one of the 24/7 counsellors there. A call can be made with the phone on loudspeaker with a child in the room to get some ideas going, modelling to the child that reaching out is helpful and normal. Remember, if an opportunity is missed, a child may ask, 'Why didn't you get me help sooner?'

Some theory

University courses may not cover child counselling in any great depth. When I speak with qualified counsellors, they commonly say, 'I'm well trained to deliver CBT, mindfulness, ACT and person-centred counselling with adults, but I've not really had the chance or gained the confidence or skills to know where to start with children'. Through a mix of theory, real-life examples and inspirational ideas, this book aims to help you fill some of these gaps in knowledge.

I have used de-identified and composite case studies, with pseudonyms to maintain privacy, to show how theories can be brought to life with children. Although I have never recorded sessions, narrative therapists often write detailed notes. These have been used, as well as my recall of the flow and focus of each case.

My intention is to avoid too much academia, allowing for this vibrant collection of creativity to swim out from these pages. However, in Appendix 1 you will find vital information about:

- duty of care to protect children
- responding to self-harm and risk
- specialist support services
- supervision.

In my experience, humour can be a helpful bridge in working with children, shining like warm sunshine into the room. Here is a funny story about a child who overcame their fear of monsters which I sometimes tell in the first session to break the ice:

Monsters under the bed

There was a young boy who had a fear of monsters under his bed at night. His knees got wobbly, and he would leap from the door to the bed, in one jump, so they would not come out and grab him before he got safely under the covers.

At last, the father phoned a counsellor, who said that his son could be cured if the boy would attend counselling every week for 10 sessions.

The father asked what the fee would be. He was told it was $100 each visit. The father frowned and did the maths. He decided it was way too much money to spend on getting rid of a foolish, childhood fear. He had an idea …

Six months later the counsellor saw the father on the street. 'Why didn't you bring your son to see me about those night-time fears?' he asked.

The father replied, 'Well, I told my son, if he could solve the problem himself, I would give him $50. The next day, I came home from work, and my son was coming down the stairs with four pieces of wood under one arm, and my saw under the other'.

The father continued, 'My son said, "Dad, I'm glad you're home. Can I have my $50?" So, I asked him, "Did you solve the problem?" and my son told me he cut the legs off the bed, so there would be no room for the monsters'.

Let the journey begin

My hope is to awaken your inner child. With a young-at-heart sparkle. That way you can graze and gather fruits from the many strategies, and adapt them to meet your client's needs, and your own style. May this book become your companion, and may you have some wonderful adventures with the children and young people who come to your door seeking support.

CHAPTER 1

Colossal Courage

'Not everything that is faced can be changed, but nothing can be changed until it is faced.'
JAMES BALDWIN

Many people hold on to a thread of hope that counselling can shine a light to help them find a pathway through their troubles. Making a decision to rock up to that first session, even if bribed, is a heroic first step. I can still recall my first time as a new counsellor. Talk about a deer in the headlights! New beginnings are both scary and exciting for everyone.

It reminds me of the Swedish word 'resfeber' which translates to:

> *'The restless race of the traveller's heart before the journey begins, when anxiety and anticipation are tangled together.'*

What happens in counselling?

There can be a mystery about counselling, especially if it is a child's first experience speaking with a professional they've never met before. Nobody likes uncertainty, so this chapter quietly and clearly covers some of the things that might happen. Of course, each counsellor will have a unique approach and style to their work, with tailored activities for individual children, young people and families.

Children are masters in the art of play. Yet trauma, fears and sadness can rob them of their spontaneity and light-heartedness. To remedy this, we can meet them in their preferred zone of fun, using playfulness to guide the child towards their imagination and resourcefulness.

In their book *Narrative Therapy in Wonderland*, authors Marsten, Epston and Markham point out that sometimes, 'the therapist might have to contribute to get the imaginative ball rolling' and 'reclaim a knack for playful communication'. They suggest 'establishing the therapy office as a welcoming site for fun'.

What is important in the child's first counselling session?

Children need a safe place in which to reflect and review what's been happening in their life. I see my role sometimes as a still mirror, reflecting back what I hear and see. I ask questions to help children think more clearly about their situation, and their sense of self, from a new perspective.

I avoid making promises about 'fixing' problems, since life brings with it many obstacles, year by year. I let young people know that I stand by them, and together we stand against The Problem. The hope is that in the future they will know how to manage difficult situations themselves, or help others, but also know that it's okay to reach out.

We must guard against being too 'friendly' or the child may consider us as a friend. We stay for just a short while in their lives, like Mary Poppins, and then, when the wind changes, we need to say goodbye. I advocate for developing authentic, compassionate warmth and having unconditional positive regard for all.

Supporting the child to make a trusting connection with the counsellor, often called the 'therapeutic alliance,' is the number one aim in the first session. We may not be given a second chance, but even if the child or family decide not to continue, the opportunity of this 'single session' has well-documented benefits for clients. A single session might lead to such sparkling ideas and new understandings about The Problem, that a family can make significant changes in their life from that first consultation.

Creating a child-centred space for a young person to tell their story, and finding out what they think might be helpful, is a great place to start.

The case study below is an example of how that first session might look, using playful and therapeutic engagement activities.

Case Study: The Tea Party - Part 1

Sasha's mum is concerned her 11-year-old daughter has performance anxiety, which is 'not diagnosed'. When she comes in for her intake appointment to provide background information, we talk about Sasha's interests and activities, including the achievements, skills and strengths that Mum is most proud of. We also create a genogram on the whiteboard and two other family members are identified as experiencing difficulties managing their worries and stress.

At the conclusion of the session, Mum says, 'It's been really nice meeting you, but I know she won't come'. So, I pull out a large sparkling red box, The Tea Party Kit. I explain, 'Sometimes it can help to bring all the family in. Tell them there's a lady who helps families when they have problems, and we'll begin with a tea party'. There are two younger children in the family, aged five and seven, and Mum agrees to ask the children to pick which foods they'd like to bring and a date is set.

The family arrives with a bag of goodies. Our receptionist, Shena, says, 'Oh you must be here for Kim's Tea Party!' Mum looks agitated but puts on a brave face. On the way to the consulting room, we stop at the kitchenette and make Mum a cup of tea.

In the room, I create an atmosphere of a special occasion as the red box is brought out, and the tiered cake stand, paper doilies, colourful plates and party hats are arranged by the children.

The children munch away and wander around, exploring the play equipment and artwork on the walls created by previous clients. Some poems and tips are also pinned to the noticeboard. Sharing stories (de-identified) from other's lived experience is a narrative therapy approach which diminishes isolation and shame. I chat with Mum and ask the children about any movies they've seen in the school holidays.

After a few minutes, I say 'So, Mum told you families come here to talk about problems. What can you see on the walls that gives you an idea about what kind of problems children might be struggling with?'

The younger children point to drawings, including one that shows two houses: 'Mum's house' and 'Dad's house'.

'That's like us!' says the seven-year-old. I say that families come here to get help with tricky problems. I ask them to see if there's any other problems in the gallery that match what's happening in their family. This gets us talking about what counselling might have to offer.

Sasha sees the emotion poster and studies the words under each image. The others run and try to read the words. Sasha reads out the feelings for them. I show them how to play a game where you choose a face and not tell anyone, but the others have to guess the feeling. We take it in turns to play 'Feelings Charades'.

(Image credit: https://www.kimochis.com/products/)

Once the emotion is guessed, then a story of when you last felt that emotion is told.

After some laughter and funny stories are told, Sasha chooses a feeling. She mimes looking down into her clutched hands and the five-year-old guesses, 'Shy?' Sasha says, 'No, it's "uncomfortable" like when I get wobble knees before I go on stage'.

I ask Mum who else in the family knows what The Wobbles feels like. (Since we discussed this in our intake, Mum was prepared.) I then ask, 'So, do Aunty Sue and Grandma sometimes shake off The Wobbles and enjoy a steady life?' This is normalising and remedying the way The Problem had previously been described in hushed tones at home as, 'Sasha's an anxious child'.

I tell the children I also sometimes get The Wobbles when I am trying a new dessert recipe (a carefully worded, appropriate 'personal disclosure'). I describe how I have a wobbly worry it might not work out, and hold my hand where I feel that uncomfortable energy, in my belly and chest. I tell them that once the dish is served, I breathe a big sigh of relief when everyone is enjoying the cake.

I draw a timeline on the whiteboard to show the different stages of my wobbles, with ample dramatisation of my hopes and fears, and ask Sasha if that was similar to hers, and she says it is. 'Maybe we could find out more about what mischief The Wobbles get up to at your place next time?' This use of a character as the problem is a narrative technique of 'externalising' which offers some much needed social distancing from a problem.

Time's up, and as I begin to pack away the plates, I ask each child what they found helpful coming in today. Sasha says, 'I feel much better talking about this. Can I come again, Mum?' Sasha's embarrassed, downwards glance has become a hope-filled beaming smile.

Conversations with parents

When meeting parents for the first time, David Epston would politely ask permission to postpone any discussion of The Problem for 20–30 minutes, saying 'I'm wondering if you could introduce me to your daughter's wonderfulness?'

I sometimes ask parents to write a letter to their children after I have asked the pivotal question, 'What do you admire about your child? What touches your heart about your child?' This way, the child is the centre of our conversations, and we push The Problem to one side whilst we find out how the parents might rally to the child's side as they face the difficult problem they have stumbled across.

My curiosity then leans into the family connection to The Problem, and I casually ask the parent, 'Oh, and did you ever have a problem with anger/stealing/lying/etc.? What birth order are you? Which of your children are you finding a breeze at the moment?'

We are consulting with people who love their child, but at present the parents may have some heightened emotions that don't feel so very warm or nurturing. I am curious about how each family member deals with stress. I want to hear anecdotes with all the details, not generalised comments. I may ask, 'What's the best thing about this family, and what's the hardest part?' or 'When you were younger, did you picture having a family looking like this? What is missing from your dream family? What is important to you? What are you most proud of about how well you've done so far?'

I may also ask if the child was conceived out of love, accidentally, or 'to save the marriage'. I would not divulge this to a child, but if the story was that the parents created a child out of love and hope, then this narrative can become a rich sense of self-worth for the child, even after divorce.

I ask about the pregnancy, birth, weaning, toilet training and developmental milestones. These may well reveal there is a history of The Problem that had been overlooked. We are looking broadly, and enquiring about the family's strengths, networks and hopes.

I usually ask, 'What might be good for me to attend to in the sessions with your child?' and 'Are you, as a family, ready, willing and capable of being there for your child while they come for a series of appointments? Do you feel confident we can work together for a few months and change the direction of this problem?' I also add, 'What is one thing you'd notice about life at home, if this problem was getting smaller?'

This is also the time to discuss confidentiality. 'Unless I think a child is at risk of harm, what we discuss in-session is private. If I think you could benefit from knowing something, I will talk about this with your child, and we may summarise and share it with you'.

Mostly, I prefer to work with the whole family, so the good work we do carries onwards into the home. I explain, 'We're working together to help your child progress through this difficult time. Consultations with you may also be helpful, and so after three or four child sessions, it might be good to book in another parent session. What are your thoughts?'

During these later parent sessions, I ask, 'How well do you think the counselling is going? Are there any concerns you have about progress? Have you noticed any changes at home?'

A common concern I hear from those I supervise is, 'Parents don't want to be paying for children to be playing'. I recommend informing parents up-front about our focus on Dan Hughes' use of PACE in therapy (playfulness, acceptance, curiosity and empathy) and explain how spending time using play-informed strategies fosters engagement and trust, which is crucial to the therapeutic process.

Parents may also worry they will have to force their child to come to counselling. I tell them we can cross that bridge when we come to it. However, when they see their child happy to attend, I've found parents are grateful for our information about the process of counselling, and for our skilled approaches.

Being authentic

Many years ago, I read a book by Virginia Axline called, *Dibs in Search of Self*. This was a pivotal moment in my child counselling career, as I realised that children have so much wisdom about what they need and thrive when they find a safe person who communicates warmth and authenticity. They soon know if they feel safe with us online or in the in-person therapy space, where their feelings, thoughts and even behaviours will be accepted.

I usually like a parent to stay for a portion of the session with younger children, especially the first one. This can be a barometer of the dynamics. If the adult tells tales on their child, or spends time correcting them, for example, 'Say thank you … Don't jump on the beanbag … Now tidy up that mess!' I may recommend the parent watches a four-minute YouTube video by Dr Gabor Maté – *Authenticity vs. Attachment* (https://youtu.be/l3bynimi8HQ).

I model and set the tone around my values of respect and free expression. I can later use what I've observed to speak with the parent in a parent session about how such correcting in public might feel for the child.

My room rules are: 'This is a safe place to express yourself in any way you want to. As long as you don't come and push me off the chair, I am pretty relaxed. Even if a toy gets broken, it's not a big deal here'.

I recall four-year-old James who kept trying to smother his two-year-old brother with the beanbag. It was the first family session and Mum was exhausted. I asked James if he would like Mum and the toddler to wait outside. He agreed, and immediately created a dynamic sand tray scene and a drawing supported by my vast sticker collection. His need to feel safe from his own rage were met through one-on-one, post-trauma therapy. On the last session some months later, the whole family came in again, and there was not a hint of hostility (see case study Chapter 7).

What is the child's understanding about counselling?

Sometimes I want to hear about what the young person thinks about counselling up-front. 'Why do you think your parent/teacher thought counselling might be a good idea? Have you heard about counselling from friends? I hope you'll let me know if it's a waste of your time, or if I'm doing your head in.'

I might say, 'I'm here to see if I can help you make sense of your problems and find ways to get through these hard times. How come you agreed to come here? What kind of help are you looking for? Do you have any new ideas about how we might work together on The Problem?'

The reluctant person

Counsellors often ask me in supervision what to do when a child doesn't want to be there. They tell me agonising stories, where a young person sits and shrugs their shoulders, mumbling, 'I dunno' and showing through their body language their disinterest and disdain for being dragged along. Remember, only 7% of communication is verbal—the majority is unspoken, with 55% delivered via body language, and 38% through tone, pauses and other effects.

Young people from 12–18 years often express their normal developmental reserve, indifference, and suspicion of 'adults'. They can harbour thoughts such as, *An adult would have NO idea about helping teenagers of today.* So my suggestion to counsellors is to start by naming that 'elephant in the room'.

'I'm guessing you might have a few doubts about where this counselling may take us, or how helpful today might be? But if we could talk for say, 20 minutes, and see how it goes, you can let me know if we're on track. Maybe you could turn on your phone timer and we can stop then, and check-in on how it's going?'

Or, if those heels are well and truly dug-in, 'I can see you're not so keen to talk. That's okay. In fact, please don't speak at all for the first five minutes. I'll give you these YES/NO buzzer buttons and you can communicate through them'. (Or, if the

session is online, 'Please hold up something red/green and I can press the buttons!')

Here's the first question: 'Were you bribed to come here today, with more computer time or a treat or something?' They naturally press the YES button, and this crazy joker voice comes out of the gadget saying 'YEEEEAH-HA-HA-HA-HA!' Next I ask, 'Was this the very first time your parents had suggested you come to counselling?' They press the NO button (every time), and a high-pitched angry voice screams out: 'I said, NO!' Soon there's some laughter in the room, and we can transition to a conversation.

Invitational conversations

If a child has experienced trauma, I attend carefully to my own, and their non-verbal body cues. I may say, 'I've heard that some sad/scary things have happened. You can talk about whatever you want to in counselling, so I will allow you to choose what we talk about.

It doesn't seem fair these things have happened to you. Maybe as we play or do some drawings, you could share your feelings about the unfairness? You can look at this emotion poster on the wall' (or on the slide if online).

I may put The Bears cards on the floor to help identify feelings. 'Can you find three or more to tell me the story of how your weekend was?' I keep it very low-key and slow to start with.

Starting with the end in mind, I may say, 'Sometimes children like to make time at the end of the session to play a game. I like balloon volleyball. What about you? Shall we set the timer to make sure we have time to play a game at the end?'

Magic tricks

I carefully consider the seriousness of The Problem I heard about at intake. If it feels appropriate to enhance that therapeutic connection with a magic trick, I have one or two up my sleeve. I ask the child if they know any magic tricks.

Not every counsellor can pull off an exciting performance. Sometimes mine go terribly wrong, and this brings a good laugh that sure breaks the ice!

Some children might not be interested in games or tricks, and think I'm wasting their time. That's fine. I welcome any and all feedback. I could invite them to set an agenda, write it on the whiteboard. I give them agency and purpose. Perhaps they'd like to write up some of their goals and hopes for the future? I embrace all dissent and demonstrate the courage to handle rejection.

However, if their eyes sparkle with interest, here's a very simple trick:

Paper clips: I open an envelope and tip six loose paperclips onto the table. 'How many are there?' (Six) I put them back in the envelope and say, 'Does anyone know a magic word?' If they don't, I ask them to google one. They say the chosen word, and I wave my hand over the envelope.

When I tip out the paperclips again, they have now become a chain of six paperclips! (See below for how this is done.)

> The magic paperclip trick is done by gluing two identical sized envelopes back-to-back. Then in one envelope, you put six loose paperclips, and add six in the other that are linked in a chain.

I share the secret of how it's done and ask them if they'd like to practise it themselves to trick a friend at school.

Here are some more competitive games for the whiteboard/on paper:

1. **Dots and boxes:** Draw a series of dots 2 cm apart to form a square grid. Each person takes a turn to draw one vertical or horizontal line, to join any two neighbouring dots. If on your turn, you can enclose a square, you write your initial inside the square, and draw another line. Then the other person has a turn. The aim is to have gained the most squares.

2. **Wordsearch:** This is less competitive than dots and boxes. We ask the child to think of a long word, then all see how many smaller words can be made using the letters. My favourite word to use is COUNSELLING—can you guess how many smaller words I have found in that 11-letter word? (There are well over 30!)

Online counselling

This has become a large part of how we work now. Much of what we did in face-to-face work is actually transferable. I can still do playful warm-up games using the Zoom whiteboard, 'scissors-paper-rock', and a few of my magic tricks. Mirroring games have also been great for focusing and getting us out of our chairs.

Engagement games might include: Get something from the kitchen, put it in a bag and I have to guess what it is using the '20 Questions' yes/no style.

I have mailed young children art pads and textas, stickers and play doh. Older children may get a stress ball and a packet of wooden craft pop sticks with a fine pen to write down their experiences, feelings, ideas, hopes and helpful self-talk onto the pop sticks and keep in two separate jars: 'The good stuff' and 'The not-so-good stuff'.

Safety and privacy requirements mean we're attending to many extra things in-session, but we can still invite the child to bring a snack, a toy or a sporting award. And of course, everyone is keen to show their pets!

I create a Virtual Art Gallery PowerPoint presentation to gather together my psych-ed resources, and images of items from around

the room. This can be personalised with a welcome page. If the child is interested in a computer game or a certain animal, I may have that as the first page with their name on it. Other slides may include examples of the kind of things we might do in sessions: brightly decorated with stock images/dog emotion pictures/symbolic images (similar to sand tray) and invite the child to share which ones they are drawn to. There may be Plutchik's Wheel of Emotions from Google images, or a psych-ed resource about depression or anxiety.

Summary

In the first session we begin to learn about each other, and explore how we might work together, and make sure we're having as much fun as is respectful. We're not yet into deep conversations about The Problem, because we're attending to what the child needs in terms of establishing a trusting, therapeutic alliance. I convey this is a safe place to talk, and demonstrate I am skilled in journeying beside young people who are experiencing feeling stuck or overwhelmed by tricky problems.

We must ask questions that stir curiosity and gets the child thinking for themselves, such as 'What is important to you?'

The counselling space might be the only really safe space, or neutral ground at this time for this young person. I offer a therapeutic connection where they can be heard and feel valued, and where their preferred identity and hopes can be restored.

Actions to take as a result of reading this chapter

1. Search on YouTube 'learn a magic trick' or 'how to play the dots and boxes game' and use these as ice breakers where appropriate.

2. Enrol in a creative therapy training webinar, such as a Zoom Whiteboard Therapy or Playful Narrative Therapy short course.

3. If you're going to be delivering sessions online, create a 'Welcome to Counselling' PowerPoint presentation with your usual resources for anxiety, depression, bullying, etc., colourfully and simply arranged on slides, accompanied with images from stock photos/stickers.

CHAPTER 2

What's Wonderful About You?

'Every story that a child tells, contributes to a self-portrait that the child can look at, refer to, think about and change.'

SUSAN ENGEL

I've spent many years working with children with different types of problems, and have learnt that most of the problems do not actually belong to them. Many problems are passed down through systemic disadvantages, poor role modelling and genetic vulnerabilities. As a counsellor, we have to accept that many of the problems we hear about cannot be 'fixed'.

Counsellor self-care

My heart still breaks at times with the suffering children endure. If ever it doesn't, that is my red flag to show me I'm experiencing compassion fatigue. We're not invincible, we're not programmed artificial intelligence machines that can be worked non-stop and feel nothing. We're not given a magic wand, tucked up inside our university degrees.

Parents, teachers and counsellors need time to recharge. We know the risks of vicarious trauma, so we need to make room for our self-care as a priority. Nobody will tap you on the shoulder, and say, 'Hey what about taking three days off, just for you, to reconnect with who you are?'

For me, narrative therapy's focus on getting to know *The Person* as separate to *The Problem* has been a helpful way to continue in this work without burnout.

Case study: Missing Mum

Jet is a 10-year-old boy living in foster care. He has a track record of unimaginable experiences leading to an identity based on street credibility. He said his problems were 'hating school' and 'missing Mum' (who Jet had supervised contact with each week, along with his three-year-old brother living in a separate home). These conversations were exploring Jet as a person, separate to the multiple diagnoses and misdemeanours he is better known for.

Kim: Has The Problem stolen all your hope for what you want?
Jet: Yes. I used to be really sure I'd be allowed to go back and live with Mum, but I'm not now. I don't think I ever will. That's why I run away to her place.
Kim: What stops you giving up on going back to live with mum?
Jet: I don't know.
Kim: What keeps you looking up?
Jet: I love it when I see my baby brother. I get to look after him.
Kim: Who's been teaching you these looking after skills?

Jet: Mum. She says 'Hey, Jet. How are you going? Are you thirsty?'
Kim: I notice you love movies. Are there some you've watched lots of times?
Jet: *Hotel for Dogs* is my favourite, it's about kids like me ... but it's really sad. (I used Bear Cards to identify sadness, anger and shame.)
Kim: How else do the kids in the film feel like you?
Jet: They keep on caring for Friday (the lost dog) and the other dogs, and putting up with people being mean.
Kim: Is 'keep on caring' another important thing that matters to you?
Jet: Mum keeps caring for me when she can. My friends look out for me, and I'll always be caring for my baby brother.
Kim: When I get here, you always ask me if I want a cup of tea! What skill would you call that? Welcoming skills?
Jet: Friendship skills. I learnt them from other kids at school. I want to be a great friend.
Kim: Could we make a certificate of recognition for your 'Looking After' and 'Keep on Caring' and 'Friendship Skills'? Who else could we make an extra copy for?
Jet: Mum! And I'll give one to Nan, and can we put one up on the welcome board here?

WHAT'S WONDERFUL ABOUT YOU?

'I cannot teach anybody anything. I can only make them think.'
Socrates

As I get to know The Problem, I need to get to know The Person. Many people think a counsellor's first task is to listen to the client's stories about The Problem. But that's only half the story. I need to know the impact of hardships, and what valiant attempts they've been making to overcome difficulties, but I mustn't get stuck in the problem story, and possibly come to feel as defeated by it as the child. Let's meet the child first.

Counselling is a safe place to hear about a child's emerging values. These life-affirming principles guide people as they decide what is right and what is wrong, and how to respond to various situations. These conversations can provide a significant counterbalance to The Problem. Such narrative therapy practices of hearing about what a child gives value to is called 'double listening'.

Personal interest questions allow the child to talk about themselves in a way that distances themselves from The Problem. Then, with a few metaphors up our sleeves, we can move into talking about The Problem as a separate, though troublesome part of their life: 'If this problem was the other basketball team you're playing against, what name would you call it? How would you prepare to meet them on the court?'

These conversations show we're coming from a place of respect and non-judgemental acceptance. I use playful therapeutic games to find out what's important to the child, and why these things are meaningful. Children then tell stories about their skills in ways that will be helpful when we step into The Hacker's Chair (see Chapter 4). This is where we put The Problem under the spotlight.

One example of a values conversation I had, was with an eight-year-old who'd been excluded, teased and pushed by another girl at school. My question was, 'Why did you choose not to push her back? Could you draw using a picture of a pizza (pie chart), the size of 'scared' and the size of 'I don't want to hurt people' and anything else you stand by? Could you tell me why you choose not to hurt people? Who else would understand this about you? What does this choice say about you and what you hope for in your life?' This is a refreshing and shame-free way to respond to bullying in the first session.

Many new counsellors can get stuck at this stage of therapy and find CBT just doesn't cut the mustard. That's why this book is in your hands today, because such resources that step us through the various stages of counselling with creative, new directions are in short supply.

Therapeutic games introducing questions

I recently learned there is even a set of Therapy UNO cards available! I'm always on the lookout for games that will help children notice and talk about their thoughts, feelings and dreams in ways that will reduce the impact of their current problem. If a child is restless, and losing focus in session, perhaps movement might be helpful. I may ask a child to choose a balloon and we can play some balloon volleyball to shake out the wriggles. Online we may both stand up and do some Mirror Moves.

WHAT'S WONDERFUL ABOUT YOU?

Below are some games I play to explore values:

1. Jenga quiz: This is where intentional therapeutic questions are selected and written on each Jenga block. For example, 'What does a team need to be successful?' or 'What is your golden rule of living?' or 'How do you encourage others?' These are narrative-informed questions to generate values and skill-based stories of the child's understanding about the world and themselves.

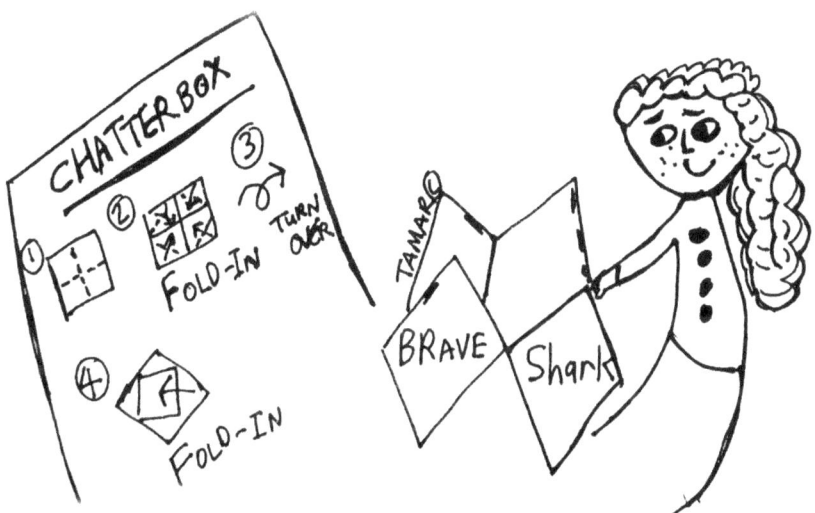

2. Chatterbox: Similar questions to the above can be written under the flaps of this age-old game. The child chooses a number/colour/sticker on a chatterbox, and there's a question: 'What have you noticed about cats?' or 'Why do people like pets?' (online and in person). The child can also fold the origami chatterbox and make one to take home. Perhaps they can add questions they would like to ask a parent, but haven't found a way to yet. (A demonstration, pattern and sample questions can be found on my website.)

3. Getting-to-know-you-box: Children can add to the collection of questions written on folded pieces of paper. Online, a child can select a number from 1–20 and then a resource PowerPoint slide in the Virtual Art Gallery can have a question written on it. We have to be up for answering a few too!

Examples of additional questions (always followed by a 'why?'):

- Who are the helpful people in your life?
- Who do you help?
- If you were principal at a school one day, what would you do differently?
- How do you recognise a person you know you cannot trust?
- What are you proud of about yourself?
- Why would you want to change anything about you?
- What has been a peak moment in your life?
- What event have you bookmarked as a particularly low moment in your life?
- Who's your (footy) team? Did they win the Grand Final last year? Why not? What stopped them being their very best? How do people make comebacks from injuries?
- If we were writing a book about your life story, what could we call the recent chapters? Would it have a chapter about the times you've cared for your brother, or helped Nan?
- Wild animal genogram: Could you find an animal from this box which represents you? Then one for Mum/Dad/siblings/Grandma/best friend/teacher, etc. Where you put them on the paper/sand tray might show me who you're close to, and who you like in your face, nose-to-nose ... and who you prefer to have some space from. How does (person) remind you of the (animal)? If your animal could speak to (person), what might it say? (See image Chapter 9.)

- The needle of this compass always points North … what is your North? What's important for you? Can you tell me a story where you've done that (helping/caring/…)? Why is that value precious to you? Who else shares that value with you?

A List of Values

Teamwork Family Kindness Honesty Caring Patience Courage Respect

Some examples of values include: teamwork, family, helpfulness, kindness, honesty, caring, creativity, generosity, patience, courage, independence, respect, calm, peace, reliability, equality, care for environment and health. This list can be used to talk about 'needs'.

With teenagers

Another engagement strategy with older children is a non-dialogue interaction, where you invite the young person to choose three or more of the following questions to introduce themselves to you, using an iPad. These questions were collated by Alice Morgan in her *Practice notes: Introducing narrative ways of working.*

- What name do you like to be called? What do you like about it?
- Is there a place that has precious memories for you? What makes that special?
- During your life, what learnings have been positive for you?
- Who is important to you and knows your special skills, qualities and values?

- How have you managed to overcome difficulties in the past? What strengths do you draw on in hard times? Who do you turn to in hard times?
- What do you think about these questions, and would it be interesting to talk more about these stories of your strengths and connections?

Managing expectations of parents

New counsellors may say, 'Parents tell me they want me to focus on eliminating The Problem and teaching the child strategies. Implying they want me to fix their child'.

In response to this we can say, 'Your child and I will be very problem-focused. I will also be "person-centred" because through my professional training, I understand the effects of stress, and will attend carefully to how your child is making sense of The Problem/trauma, and what ideas they have about steps forward'.

Perhaps we can ask the parent to reflect on the times and places where they get to breathe out. Where for a while, their own identity is separate to their personal problems. We can talk about the healing properties of laughter, and safe spaces to be themselves, and how children also strive for this same freedom and acceptance, especially when there are stressful life transitions, scary problems or unpleasant people in their lives.

Our role includes connecting with the child or young person, so they sense our enjoyment of life and their company. We can develop ways to be mindful in-session, with our own style of authentic curiosity and warmth.

WHAT'S WONDERFUL ABOUT YOU?

*'We don't stop playing because we grow old,
we grow old because we stop playing.'*
George Bernard Shaw

Identity

Children are busy constructing and comparing their emerging self to those around them. The story they tell themselves is often in relation to how they feel they measure up to other people's expectations and accomplishments around academic success, social and family status, sporting skills, appearance, etc. Under the weight of a big problem, their self-esteem can be diminished, and this can lead to negative identity conclusions.

In narrative therapy we use externalising language (explored in Chapter 3) to gain some separation from the problem. I may say, 'Children tell me that problems can be very annoying. That problems can make you think there's something wrong with you. They say problems can sometimes make it hard for you to have fun. What do you think?'

We can learn how a child is making sense of their world and what they believe from listening to how they tell their story. In the case of Jet, his values around being a good friend and caring for his brother are important to him. Our conversations allowed him to voice his care, to counterbalance the dominant problem story told about him by others. This shapes the emerging understanding the child has of who they are, where they fit in and what might be possible for them.

Such approaches are 'strength-based' and in taking the theory into practice, we need to avoid making 'congratulatory' statements such as, 'Oh you have so many strengths. You're doing so well'. Instead, we can form questions which invite the child to reflect and think about what talking about these values means for them. 'If you were to stay connected to your values of friendship and caring, what would that mean to you?'

Hearing the voice of the child

Using the child's exact words and phrases shows the importance of privileging the child's voice. For example, 'Would you like to write about this in this Wisdom Book, where other children have offered their tips and success stories?' or 'I'd like to take a photo of that drawing/graph/timeline and keep it for your file. Are you okay with that, and would you like me to print you a copy? Would you like it to be private, or up on the wall for others to look at?' With parental consent, I may add a drawing to a virtual gallery PowerPoint online, and there is a virtual wisdom jar that can also be used.

In narrative therapy, we openly take notes in session to write the exact phrases a child uses. I show my notes to the child if they ask. I might say, 'Can I write down, "my cat is precious to me"? It sounds important to you. What is it about your cat that makes you feel this way? Can you tell me a story about how that preciousness came to be? Would the cat also say you were precious to him? Did you just wake up one day and know it, or is there a family tradition or story of connecting with cats?'

I've also learnt how powerful a pet can be in the life of a child. A whole family I was working with once stopped arguing completely when their dog died.

I like to ask children, 'Here's a BIG question. How come Mum and Dad made you three children, but you all do things in life differently?

WHAT'S WONDERFUL ABOUT YOU?

Each of you has slightly different ideas of what's right, and what's not right. You all like different things: food, sport, activities. So how have you been shaping who you are becoming as a unique person? What thoughts are guiding you?'

By using their imagination, we can invite children to picture a time in the future, when they'll have more power. 'When you're a dad one day, what three things have you learnt that are important that you might want to remember?' These questions around possible futures are ways to achieve one of narrative therapy's aims to explore the child's preferred ways of living. Their answers can be written inside a rolled cardboard time capsule.

> *'The two things in life you are in total control over are your attitude and your effort.'*
> **Billy Cox**

Case study: Using strength cards

Strengths Cards® can be used with all ages, and online you can create a few PowerPoint pages using stock images and a few key words. I may ask what strengths a child's favourite fictional character has, such as Woody from Toy Story—loyal, caring, smart? Or even Incey Wincey Spider—determined, patient, clever?

This is how I used them with 11-year-old Dani who had been experiencing bullying from a previous friendship group:

Kim: Here are some cards, could you choose a few that really tell me about some of your strengths? Then can you tell me a story of when you recently acted using that strength. (Once selected, Dani begins to tell an anecdote from the first one.)

Dani: I am **very** patient. I had to wait for my mum to settle my baby brother for an hour last night before she could help me with my homework.

Kim: So, it sounds like patience comes in handy for you. There may be times when you run out of it, but that might be a good thing to let people know they have gone too far. Could you tell me why you think patience is an important value?

Dani: It's important because things don't always go the way you want them to, and then you can stay cool. (I am now looking for the history of this strength and value.)

Kim: When do you think you started learning about these things? Were you able to stay cool and patient in kindergarten? Is there someone else in your family who also has mastered this skill of staying cool? Dad or Gran?

In narrative practice these approaches form part of 're-authoring' conversations. I might say, 'You've come to counselling with a pocketful of problems, but I want to ask you, "What's in the other pocket?" I'm guessing there will be a bunch of hidden skills and ideas that could be useful to tackle The Problem'. This helps the child think about who they are in new and exciting, strength-based ways.

Summary

Narrative practice is founded on an appreciation that identity development is a lifetime project, and that problems can wear down a child's self-esteem. This knowledge is our reminder to take time to get to know The Person and their wonderfulness, as we hear The Problem story. This will enhance the therapeutic alliance, giving the young person a refreshing break from the often relentless feeling of personal failure.

We listen out for sparkling stories about The Person, and can use scales to notice how they balance against the stories of The Problem.

Actions to take as a result of reading this chapter

1. Take some time out to reflect or book a counselling session for yourself. Are you up to talking with a therapist about your own parent's expectations of you when you were growing up?

2. Recall the names or labels attributed to you at home or school. What was the meaning, then, and now? (See Chapter 9.)

3. Buy a Jenga tower and use it to answer some of the client questions for yourself.

CHAPTER 3

Introduce Me to the Problem

'The problem is the problem, the person is not the problem.'
MICHAEL WHITE & DAVID EPSTON

In narrative therapy, we like to put The Problem under the spotlight. We can look for clues about what a problem has been getting up to. Usually it's mischief and mayhem. Then we may look for the history of The Problem, the size of The Problem and the effects of The Problem. What emerges are the times when this problem has been held back by something a child has done. Some days The Problem seems to be having a sleep-in, and the young person gets some relief. There may be certain times or places when The Problem doesn't get a look-in. There's so much for child counsellors to explore. In narrative therapy, these other stories are called 'alternative stories'.

But first, we find ways to 'externalise' The Problem. By being able to point to it figuratively, The Person is no longer defined as inherently being The Problem. This technique repositions the child in a playful way, which motivates them to face difficulties more boldly. It works for adults, too.

Michael White first played with externalising in the 1980s and wrote up his case in the *Family Systems Medicine* journal. He began exploring how 'Sneaky Poo' (aka encopresis/faecal soiling) had come to dominate a family's life. Questions he began sculpting included:

- Are you more the boss over the Sneaky Poo, or is he more the boss over you?
- How often does Sneaky Poo spoil the day?
- How often can you put it where you want to?

Case study: Why are Mummy and Daddy not together?

Sam's Mum had been attending post-separation support sessions with me when she raised concerns about her son's behaviour. 'It is out of control. He is refusing to accept the separation and has regressed to having daily angry tantrums, hitting me and crying "Why, Mummy?" all the time.'

I suggested she bring him in, which surprised her as he had only just turned three. On arrival, Sam clutched a silkie comfort bunny. As he tentatively explored the room, his mum and I talked about some of the happy things Sam had been doing recently.

Kim: Sam, you've been to the zoo with Nanny and Mum! What are your favourite animals?
Sam: I like tigers and penguins.
Kim: Do they live together, in the same enclosure?
Sam: No!
Kim: Why not?
Sam: That would be scary for the penguin! (Sam finds a miniature tiger and penguin in a box on the shelf.)

Kim: But what if one night the zookeeper forgot that. (I put the penguin and the tiger into a smaller box together.) What if he put the penguin in with the tiger, in the same pen! And then locked up for the night, and went home?

Sam: (With a startled and worried look) The penguin would have to run ... and climb the fence and get out! (Sam dramatises the escape, lifting the penguin out and scrambling it up the chair Mum was sitting on, before hopping down the other side.)

Kim: Let's draw a picture on the whiteboard, of what's best for the penguin and the tiger. Then we can tell the zookeeper to NOT do that again. (I drew two houses, with front doors and windows. Sam drew a squiggly penguin in one and a tiger in the other.)

Kim: Now, which house is Mummy's, and which house is Daddy's?

Sam: That's Mummy's (Sam pointed to the penguin's house) and that one's Daddy's.

Kim: Sam, do you think that could be why your Mummy and Daddy are living in separate houses?

Sam: Yes! They are not friends anymore. (Sam smiled and sprang into a little hop, as he went to explore the room further.)

Mum reported in her next session that now Sam was more settled, and more his usual self. The use of symbolism, imagination, and what-if was engaging and child-centred. The problem was externalised by using the zoo metaphor, and through conversation and drawing. The outcome was a developmentally appropriate understanding and resolution to the question of 'Why are Mummy and Daddy not together?'

Metaphors

Metaphors can shift the conversation to a safer place. They join up the left and right brain, to help us step across a bridge into our imaginative mind. The metaphor image invites a new way to see a problem and opens up new possibilities.

One successful activity using a metaphor is The Juggler. I ask the young person to draw a juggler with six balls in the air, and to write the names of three problems and three fun things into them. Now we can ask which is the trickiest ball, and the one they would like to work on, to make life a bit easier.

Metaphors allow us to talk about problems at a distance, making complex situations more understandable. They might not however, work easily with children with Autism Spectrum Disorder (ASD) who may take things literally.

Case study: Katy and The Worries

Katy is a 10-year-old girl with ASD who is struggling with anxiety and worrying about what has happened, and what might happen. Her dad told me there had been a minor incident when he was with Katy walking their dog, Lucas. An aggressive, smaller dog made Katy and Lucas uncomfortable. I asked Katy, 'The next day, was Lucas still excited to go on his usual walk?' She said he was. I asked why. When she couldn't think, I suggested 'Maybe Lucas doesn't let The Worry problem get settled in his head?'

We decided dogs don't spend all their downtime at home thinking about what might have happened, and what might happen tomorrow. We mimed sitting like a dog, being alert, relaxing with a bliss face, playing with a ball, then some aggressive, snarly role play! Katy said she will ask her friends at school if their dogs also have a bliss face because they shoo away The Worries. 'Feel your tummy now. Are The Worries smaller now? What is your body saying to you when you have a bliss face?'

Lucas likes balls, so I invited Katy to use a sensory ball to squeeze, to remind her to open the door to being playful like Lucas and to let go of The Worries and find her bliss face. It was a 'bottom-up' (going from movement to talking) and so a neurologically helpful sensory item suggestion. Previously, Katy had not wanted squeezy sensory toys. I reminded her that when something scary happens, she can also seek out some reassurance from her parents, just like she would give Lucas a pat to calm him down in a thunderstorm. We found other animal metaphors after this, and Katy started to look forward to our animal talks to learn how to manage her problems in an active and enjoyable way.

Case study: Pressure to learn

Many children are brought to counselling because their parents want anger to stop. We can get curious about anger. Chris is a 10-year-old who was brought to counselling because 'He's been getting angry and resisting doing as he's told'. Chris said The Anger is worse when he's taken to after-school tutoring, and has to do all the extra homework tasks they set. He attends four tutorials a week.

After some exploration, Chris provided a closer description of The Problem, from his point of view. He called it 'The Pressure to Learn'.

I asked Chris, 'Why is this Pressure to Learn a problem?' He said it made his parents cross at him, and he was doing his best. 'So, is doing your best something that you believe in? Is this pressure making it hard to keep doing your best?' Chris agreed.

We drew a graph of a typical 24-hour day to externalise the pressure. The rage he was reaching in the afternoon was off the chart. Chris was happy to show his dad the timeline drawing, as the problem was now separate from himself.

I was concerned for his high levels of stress hormones. This changed the whole conversation, and a family meeting was held to talk about the history of this inter-generational pressure. Chris was coached by me to negotiate a deal with his parents for two days less of the tutoring, and everyone had a win. They called the process we went through as 'New Family Respecting', and they began family meetings. (See Chapter 12.)

How are problems named?

We may hear a parent or teacher name the problem as if it were connected to the child's nature: 'He's lazy' or 'She's angry' or 'She is bedwetting again' or 'They're rude'. These descriptions suggest a child and The Problem are tangled into one. More importantly there's usually a weight of judgement and frustration in the tone.

The parent-child power dynamics can create emotional battles as each attempts to regain status. Parents perform all sorts of bad behaviours themselves, in their desperate attempts to control everything. Their reactions can bring blame and shame to the child. Shame used by parents leaves a child with an unspoken question, 'Am I loved?'

Children wander into problem territories. Life's like that. But when everyone is pointing to the child's behaviour, this can initially silence the child, but then they adopt a defensive posture, to protect themselves from the secondary trauma of being yelled at by parents. What a mess!

We can take an inventory of all the problems, and so externalise them objectively. 'What problems have come to your place? I wonder how many different problems there are in the world, even? Yelling problems? Bedtime problems? Computer problems? Monster problems? Night Worries …?'

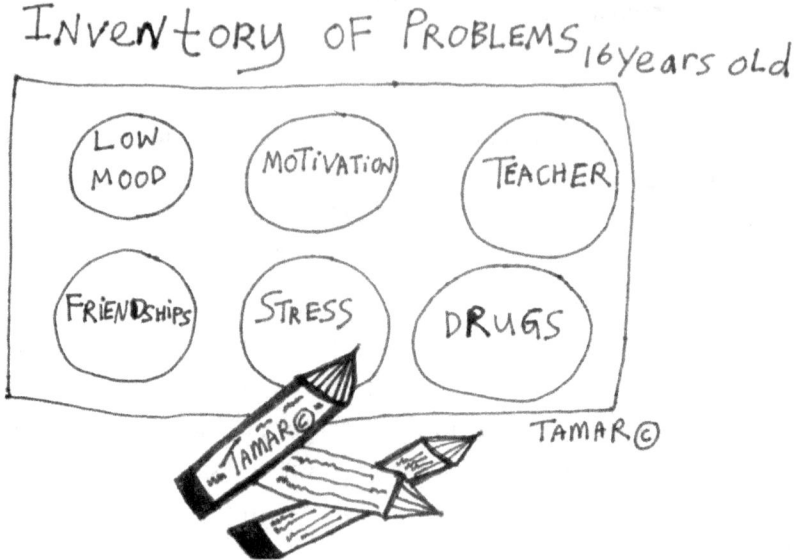

How to begin externalising the problem

Narrative therapy uses a simple linguistic device: you add the word 'the' in front of the words the person is using to describe The Problem. This describes the problem as a noun, (rather than a verb to describe behaviour or an adjective describing the person). This allows the child to begin to observe The Problem from a new angle.

Case examples

'So, Alex, it seems "The Bedwetting Problem" has become a regular visitor to your house? That doesn't sound fair. What do you think?' Nine-year-old Alex becomes curious and fired-up about this injustice and repositions herself *against* The Problem, rather than seeing herself *as* The Problem. She looks less humiliated, especially once we google the statistics.

INTRODUCE ME TO THE PROBLEM

In creating this book, someone asked me why there's a picture of a phone on the cover of a book about child counselling? I said, 'Oh, the phone is my favourite resource! In session, we might research how many teenagers struggle with anxiety. We look in the thesaurus for alternative names for a problem. Everyone seems to love checking out Google Images for metaphors to better represent The Problem. Have you researched the statistics of bullying in Australia?'

When Alex searched on my phone, she found: 'Bedwetting is very common, with 1 in 5 children experiencing bedwetting'. This shifted her shame and sense of isolation.

Sixteen-year-old Michelle's mood was sliding towards depression. She had been receiving unkind feedback from her new boyfriend. I asked, 'How has Constant Criticism injured the relationship?' and 'How is Depression spoiling your life? Have you been considering any plans to reduce Depression's influence?' We continued for a few months, abuse was also identified (see Appendix 1), and our work concluded with The Tree of Life expressive arts activity (see Chapter 11).

A puppet or dinosaur/monster toy might be chosen to represent The Problem, to more playfully talk about what is NOT GOOD about having this problem in your life. Children can create a cheer squad of toys that will stand up to the problem with them.

Another activity to try is making a cardboard weaving loom and threading different colours of wool. Life has many threads which represent the different experiences. I have a basket of wool and invite children to choose colours to represent each story. 'We could make a small plait you could turn into a wrist band, using colours to represent happy times we have talked about, as well as the challenges if you wish.'

I am guided on how to begin these conversations by the child's age and interests. With a six-year-old who has been afraid of spending time without his mum, I said, 'On the journey of life there may be a few problems. Lots of folktales are about people facing powerful enemies, like the troll under the bridge. The billy goats have a big problem because the troll is making the three billy goats afraid to cross the bridge, to get to the green grass. Can you draw your journey and name the problems challenging you? What is under your bridge?'

Narrative therapists delight in finding fun ways of naming problems (and solutions) such as 'Mr Mischief,' 'The House of Tempers,' or 'Tiger Strength'. The next step is to invite the imagination to join in: 'What might happen if everyone united against Yelling, instead of Yelling keeping everyone separated? How does Yelling get in the way of fun? How much are you wanting Yelling to learn to read: *'You're NOT welcome here?'* Shall we start by making the sign?'

Sometimes a painful event can be externalised. One 11-year-old boy chose to call his time of significant traumatic loss, 'The Worst Week'. By making reference to this, the trauma is acknowledged, and the problem could be discussed more openly. 'So, if you were to write a book about your life, and chapter two was "The Worst Week", what was happening in chapter one? Tell me about yourself and those happier times. What special memories from before might you want to recover and not let The Worst Week rob you of? How will you hold on to those precious saved treasures?' Then a name can be found for the treasures.

Scale everything—it is the narrative therapy superpower!

We cannot assume to know the size of The Problem. With a four-year-old, I might say, 'I'm thinking of Goldilocks and the three different-sized bowls of porridge … Is The Problem at school/home a tiny baby-bear-size problem? Middle-sized problem? Or a great big problem?'

Children see something new when they draw their problems using a pizza/pie chart metaphor. This also works well with an online whiteboard, and sometimes I suggest they draw two pizzas. One is for the tricky stuff, and one for the cool stuff. At the end of counselling, they can draw another, and we can see what has changed.

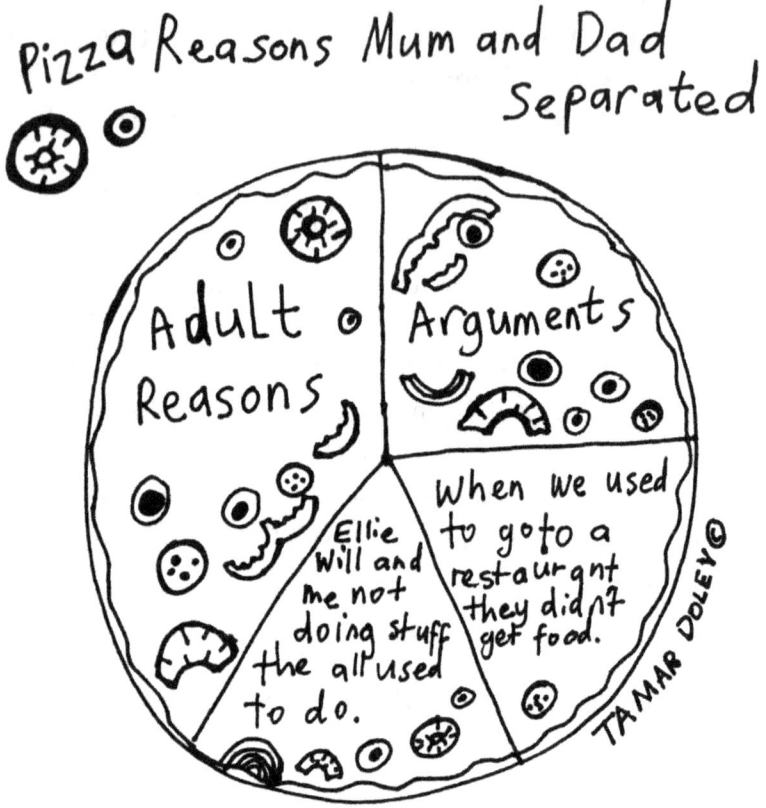

Externalising invites honest and open conversations. 'What is Anger telling you? Can Anger leap up to 10 in one jump, or do you sometimes notice Anger stepping up: 2 … 4 … 6 … 8 …? Would it be possible to be kind to this Anger before he gets to the sixth step? Are you happy with Anger being the sprinting champion, or have you something up your sleeve to beat him in his own game?' One savvy eight-year-old said, 'Kim, you can't go from zero to 10 on one jump, because if you hit 10, you were probably on five all day …'.

How to explore the history of the problem

'If you could travel back in time, in Dr Who's TARDIS, or using Star Trek's Enterprise warp 5 technology, to a favourite memory from the past, where would you go? What was happening? Who was with you? Was the problem smaller back then?'

Further enquiries can be made in a family session, such as, 'I wonder if this Drug/Anger Problem used to visit Mum or Dad's house when they were younger?' And so our investigation into the history, tricks, persistence and weaknesses of The Problem leaves no stone unturned.

The list of question prompts is endless, but counsellors tell me they love to be able to choose from a few ideas to get them started: 'How do you think your problem might have started? Who noticed it growing? How might it end? Can you look in your crystal ball? What's your prediction for it being around when you're an adult? Has this problem a use-by date? Did it suddenly arrive last week, or was it growing month by month? Is it a low, moderate or catastrophic problem?'

I tell this short story about an oak tree:

> *Did you ever hear of someone opening their front door one morning, and seeing a fully-grown oak tree in their garden? (I act out the surprise!) ... Now, big trees grow from tiny acorns... An oak tree might take 100 years to grow. That's four generations!*
>
> *Like a tree, big problems can also take a long time to grow. Sometimes they put down BIG roots into the ground. If you wanted to move that tree, you may need a few people to help pull The Problem up by the roots. Sometimes problems arrive at your front door, I wonder how they know your address. They may be delivered by the Cosmic Amazon Delivery Service ... but there's no sender's details ... it's a mystery, but we can do some tracing if you're interested?*

More questions that help externalise the problem

- What first two lines of a rap song would convey the type of problem this is?
- If The Problem was to get a bit worse, what would you call it then?
- If you could look The Problem in the eye, what would you see?
- Is this problem an uninvited guest that may just come back and visit again down the track?
- If you got to say 'goodbye!' to this problem, is there another in the queue waiting for your attention?
- If you were to paint The Problem, what colours would you be reaching for? What would you call the painting?

Case Study: The Tea Party - Part 2

Mum and 11-year-old Sasha come for the second session and after a very brief check-in, I invite Sasha to draw the journey of her connection with The Wobbles around performances. I ask if it was a bit like my graph from last week. Sasha carefully draws the graph, changing colours for the different words, and then tells the story of how when she plays the violin at home, she's not scared. Then, at rehearsal The Wobbles arrive! Sasha's slowly ascending line goes very steep. I ask for a lot of detail, and Sasha says that when she's on stage, she's the most scared, and worried.

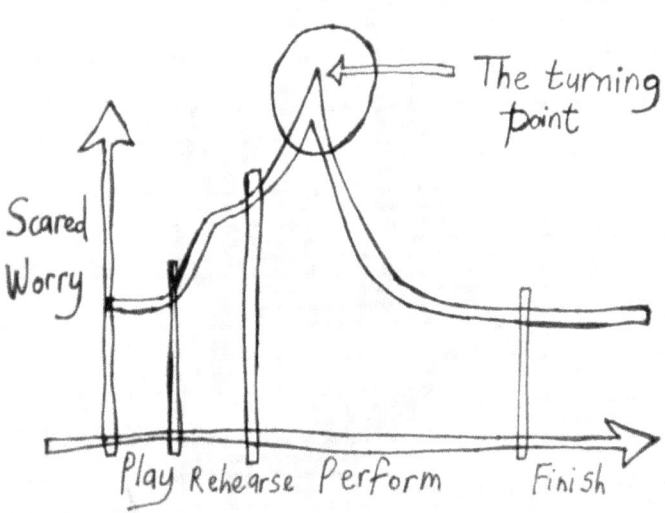

I ask if on the day of the performance when The Wobbles arrive if they are winning and grinning? Mum adds that there's a few tears, but that Sasha always manages to get into the car and then onto the stage. I ask, 'Even though you feel wobbly and scared, you still get up there! How do you do that?'

Sasha says, 'Well, I know I can do it, and I really do like to play for people. My Grandma and Pop always come and watch, so I can't let them down. Then, once I've begun, I get this really happy feeling, and I know it will be fine'.

I ask if at that turning point, The Wobbles suddenly notice Happy Feeling's presence, and know they were defeated? No longer grinning, maybe? I invite Sasha to draw a picture of this final defeat. She draws herself on stage, and just a disappearing tail of The Wobble Monster. He was last seen, running off with his tail between his legs. Sasha is so pleased, and agrees, saying that after the applause, there's never any sign of The Wobbles.

Sasha came back for one more session. In the lead-up to a competition, The Wobble Monster arrived as expected, as she had drawn in her timeline. However, this time he didn't bother her as much. Sasha said she just looked at it all differently. She was anticipating the changes and recalled the moment when her wobbly tummy and tight shoulders relaxed, not long into the performance, and the Happy Feeling arrived.

I suggested we create a certificate of 'Sasha's Outperforming The Wobbles'. Sasha illustrated it with her wearing a Happy Feeling T-shirt. The Wobble Monster's tail was added at one side of the paper, making its hasty retreat. Sasha had moved from performance anxiety to performance celebration.

Sasha wrote in the Wisdom Book I keep on my shelf for other children to read:

'Worries can make your knees shake, but when you like what you do, you can shake off the worries and get on with it to find your happy feeling.'

In the tradition of narrative therapy's acknowledgement practices, I thanked Sasha for helping me draw my own recipe graph at our first meeting. I reported that I too, was checking-in for signs of the wobbles in my belly when I was in the kitchen cooking for visitors.

Here is a story about a person who had some problems ...

The Servant at the Palace

There was once a servant at the palace, who had a scarred face as a result of a childhood illness. As such, they were dismissed by many, and always ordered around, bossed by the senior servants who were bossed by the butlers, who took orders from the ministers, who took orders from the Queen.

The servant's life seemed ordered until one day, whilst carrying out a task in the palace garden, the servant noticed a small door in a garden wall which they had not noticed before.

With curiosity, the servant turned the handle and pushed the door open. Stepping inside, the servant found a walled and disused garden, and in the centre was a dried-up fountain. After a few minutes looking around, the servant left, with a sense of hope, and returned to the chores.

The next day, and the next, and the next, the servant visited that garden, without knowing why, and tidied and weeded and set the place to rights. No-one else seemed to be aware of the place, and oddly, no-one noticed the servant was missing. Perhaps that was because the servant always finished their jobs more speedily after visiting the garden.

One day the servant noticed tiny blue and yellow flowers blooming, which the servant tended carefully. After more time, the trees blossomed and pretty red fruits began to ripen, each tasting delicious, though the servant did not know what they were.

All this brought an inner confidence, and this led to a promotion, which meant the servant was now giving orders, which they did fairly and with compassion. Promotion led to promotion, and at last the servant became a trusted counsellor to the royal family.

In the secret garden one day, the servant looked into the fountain and realised that a stone was blocking it. The servant reached forwards and removed it, and at once, water jetted out, washing all the scars from the servant's face, since it was the healing water of life.

The servant put some of this water in a bottle and proceeded to use it at the palace and elsewhere, secretly healing as and when they could, always keeping a bottle with the water in their pocket.

©Parkinson, R. (2009). *Transforming tales: How stories can change people.* Jessica Kingsley Publications.

Reproduced with permission of the Licensor through PLSclear.

Summary

Our task is to help the child describe the situation from their perspective. Having the child introduce us to The Problem using narrative practices allows us to find out what the child is thinking and feeling about it.

When The Problem is put in the spotlight, everyone sees it in a new light. Children feel the relief from shame when the whole family collectively acts to redress pre-existing and faulty negative identity conclusions. Family members can begin healing after struggles with entrenched, trans-generational patterns.

Actions to take as a result of reading this chapter

1. Look for metaphors in the world that could represent typical problems. Find free stock images to create a resource: a car stuck in the mud, a tree in winter, mending a broken toy, pulling out weeds, a teddy with a bandage.

2. Read the story the *Servant at the Palace* and ask yourself, 'How did the servant respond to their problem? What strengths and metaphors were woven into the story?'

3. Research Eugene Gendlin's focusing, where you can look for physical sensation of change, something emerging in the body's response to an emotion or thought when a problem arises.

CHAPTER 4

Hacking the Problem

'Where is the book in which the teacher can read about what teaching is? The children themselves are this book. We should not learn to teach out of any book other than the one lying open before us and consisting of the children themselves.'

RUDOLF STEINER

To remind everyone I am not an expert in their lives, I often say, 'I've only known you for one hour and 30 minutes of your life, so I have no idea what might work! But like a challenging maths problem, if you like, we could work on this together'.

DISCLAIMER: It is not this book, but the child or young person before you, who will inspire and guide you to create the approach and interventions best suited to that particular child.

Children often feel their situation is way beyond their control. The Problem may have dug itself deep in their lives, but they would not have sat back and done nothing. Like a sleuth, we can begin looking for clues where they exercised some personal agency. There are always weaknesses in The Problem's domination of their life, and we can watch out for turning points when the child got the better of The Problem. Times when the child showed bravery in the face of trouble, even if they were not able to remove The Problem. Our role is to stand with the child and hopefully find ways to hack The Problem.

'How do you get through hard times?' is a standard narrative line of enquiry leading to re-authoring conversations. The person's response is filled with their choices and values, and point to preferred identity renewals which can be charted on maps and drawings.

Some other possible opening questions include:

- What special powers or resources can you call on when faced with big problems?
- What is the history of these powers, skills and strengths?
- Who else would know this about you?
- What might they say about you if they were sitting here today?

'Children are not strangers to trauma...
No child is a passive recipient of trauma, regardless of the nature of this trauma. Amongst other things, children take action to minimise their exposure to trauma and to decrease their vulnerability to it by modifying the traumatic episodes they are subject to, or by finding ways of modifying the effects of this trauma on their lives. However, it is rare for children's responses to the traumas of their lives to be acknowledged.'
Michael White (2005)

Case study: Olivia knows how to be a friend

Olivia is eight years old and struggling with 'friendship problems'. She knows all the ideas about how to be a good friend, as her parents and teachers have told her these many times. The last thing a counsellor should do is join the advice-giving brigade. I always ask, 'What kind of advice have people given you about this problem?'

Olivia rolls off the list: you need to listen, take turns, include everyone, be nice and don't get angry. I ask, 'Which of these is most helpful for you? Why is it an important tip? Which of these is your 10/10 top friendship skill? Which one might be a bit lower down on the score?' Olivia draws a pizza/pie chart to scale her strongest ones. 'Why do you think the "Include Everyone Problem" is a problem for you?' Olivia's answers reflect how each of these tips align with her own values about friendship.

We don't have to 'coach' Olivia, she actually has the answers within. The narrative-style questions assist people to discover what they think is of value, what they may want to do about a problem, and what might be the stumbling blocks.

More metaphors

I am not quite as tech savvy as I'd like to be, but I like using hacker terminology with teenagers. We get to talk about how hackers need to know their target well. The process of gathering information about a target is known as enumeration, so I suggest we could gather information about The Problem. We often make this quite formal by charting it in a table, so it's perfect for Zoom whiteboard use. We can identify the vulnerabilities or weak points of The Problem, and consider ways to compromise its power base.

My belief is that if you can find a metaphor to work with, there will be a shift in the way a client (of any age) sees their position in relation to The Problem. In narrative therapy, this is called 're-positioning'. I encourage a child to draw a picture or score the power dynamics of the impact of The Problem in their life. Then, the changes in their Ninja skills are made visible, and The Problem's influence can be seen to be diminishing.

One avid Harry Potter fan used the 'Riddikulus' spell to disable The Problem. Every time the Bully (who'd been mimicking his speech) appeared, he pictured them as a great big ugly parrot, chained to a perch, with bald patches and a floppy wing. We discovered that humour and fear cannot co-exist.

In the case studies below, I've used metaphors, Dr Google and charts to record and measure the scores of the child versus The Problem, and found externalised names for problems, alternative stories and solutions.

Single session success

The key to this work is to recruit the child's imagination and brainstorming powers. For them, anything is possible. Five-year-old Pip had been tyrannising her three-year-old sister and was brought in to find out what was going on. In our first session, Pip discovered her own alternative story, seemingly out of thin air and said, 'I'm saying hello to the Kindness Habit!' She drew a picture of her and her sister together playing, and promptly became the model big sister much to everyone's surprise. I asked her how she made that decision. 'The people I like are the kind ones, my teacher, my mum and you. I don't want to be the mean girl anymore'. Pip had found her own solution story.

Another memorable example of spontaneous, single-session solution magic was by four-year-old Bryson. His parents had been having trouble reassuring and settling Bryson after nightmares.

Bryson drew some crazy, scribbly dreams on paper. He asked his dad to write what he will say to them every night before bed: 'Poo poo, bum bum to the Bad Dreams'. We created a plan to uninvite Bad Dreams from their home. That night, a plate was added at the dinner table, with only a teeny portion for The Bad Dreams. The next night, the plate was left empty. The following night, the empty plate was put by the front door, and after that it was left at the letter box. Bryson said he thought it would work because 'there's always a happy ending'. (He had watched *Toy Story*.)

The following week Bryson's parents booked a session for their nine-year-old daughter, Mia who had recently been diagnosed with a serious medical condition. She was struggling with a fear of needles and pills that had become part of her life, and it was interrupting her confidence going to school camp. I asked Mia to draw up a chart on the whiteboard and everyone had to write something they found fun, something they were afraid of and some compassionate self-talk they could whisper in their own ear to help them through tricky moments.

Name	Fun and 😊 Courageous Things	Not so fun things and Scary stuff ☹	Self talk messages
Mum	New Job	Knee injury	"It will all be better soon"
Dad	Camping	Scared of doing presentations at work.	"Prepare Well!"
9 year old	New cousin New friend	Tablets and blood tests	"My friend and family are always here for me"

Tamar Dolev ©

This single session again worked for Mia, because everyone was capable and willing to make changes to get rid of troubling problems. At first Mia could not think of what to whisper, but Dad said he would say to himself, 'Prepare well!' and then he would have more confidence with his presentations. Mum had a knee injury that was stopping her going to the gym, and chose 'It will be better soon'. After a few minutes, Mia wrote up her self-talk: 'My friends and family are always here for me'.

Two months later, the parents reported Mia had shifted from fear to confidence, and Bryson was still using his age-appropriate creativity to solve problems that came his way.

Working with teenagers around anxiety

There are many professionals and organisations with user-friendly, accessible information for finding ways to hack problems, and many are informed by neuroscience. I like to have an iPad ready and invite young people to search for Black Dog (https://www.blackdoginstitute.org.au/) and other useful resources, such as Insight Timer (https://insighttimer.com/) a free app for sleep and anxiety. We then talk about the impact of various problems and go from there. Karen Young also offers interesting free, psych-ed material for young people on her website Hey Sigmund (https://www.heysigmund.com/), including a great article, *Anxiety in Teens – How to Help a Teenager Deal With Anxiety.*

I recommend counsellors listen to some of Dr Gabor Maté's YouTube videos to gain a better understanding of anxiety and its origins as an adaptive response from childhood. He explains that fear is a survival attachment alarm, when a child's needs are not being met. The child then cries to bring the parent, just as a kitten meowing brings the mother cat who provides timely, responsive care.

He suggests that in our increasingly isolated, impersonal society, children are often away from a safe-haven and can sense a general threat or an absence of protection. Their fear response, which is a normal survival mechanism, is made worse when belonging needs are not met. Anxiety is then the desperate cry of a smaller part of ourselves, where fear from earlier years and accumulated unmet needs come together. I use the babushka doll as a symbol of this small self.

What are the principles and beliefs that may guide us in this work?

Every now and then, I find a quote that shifts my mind—it resonates with me because they have put into words what I was sensing. What have you seen, or read about recently that gave you a sign you were on track? For me, Milton Erikson's words about what is helpful have become one of my guiding principles, and relevant to my approach to the notion of co-creating 'alternative stories'.

Erikson believed: '... *in an unwavering belief in the client's self-healing capabilities ... intensely focused on the client's views of their concerns, their goals for therapy, and their ideas about change.*'

He also said: '*It's not what you do, it's not what you say, but what the patient does, what the patient understands that matters.*'

Case study: Leena's growing up project

Eight-year-old Leena came to see me due to her 'School Refusal'. At intake, her parents said they were embarrassed and angry to be carrying the burden of shame.

Leena had not been into a classroom for five months. Sometimes they dragged her to the school gates, but Leena would literally dig those heels in. (This was before the home-schooling of lockdown, which would have suited Leena very nicely.)

In the family session, I asked Leena to be our minute taker using the whiteboard. On the left in red, were words about The Problem, and on the right in green, were words that seemed to dispute The Problem's attempt to make the family feel like a failure.

The red list included yelling, screaming, swearing, dragging to the car, etc. The green list included Leena helping out with the laundry and in the kitchen, taking their dog on walks with Dad each evening, going to bed without a big fuss, cuddles with Mum, and nobody ever turning to hitting. This was what is called, a sparkling moment, as there before our eyes was a shining thread of respect. I asked what that meant, that no matter what, they would never hit. They added 'we love each other' in the green list.

Everyone agreed the label of 'School Refusal' was a problem. I invited the family to choose a comeback name, since the green list was quite extensive. After some discussion, 'Leena's Growing Up Project' was chosen.

I asked Leena why this fresh start was helpful for her, pointing out that she was even looking a bit taller and grown up, just writing that name on the whiteboard. Leena said she was excited at the idea of her taking charge of getting up in the mornings. 'I know I need Mum and Dad, but I don't need their help all the time.'

Leena said that if she had enough time to get dressed and have breakfast, without being rushed, she would feel less jittery about being driven by angry parents to the school, where battle #4 (getting out of the car) would begin. (Battle #1 was identified as getting out of bed, #2 getting dressed and #3 leaving the house.)

When Leena said she wanted to buy an old-fashioned alarm clock that rings as her solution to getting up earlier, her parents seemed to find every reason why that wouldn't work. They insisted they could simply knock on her door and wake her up at that time. I started to see how Leena's ideas were not taken seriously.

I suggested that there was no harm in taking up Leena's suggestion and trying this experiment for one week. Mum and Leena googled the cost of such a clock, and we brainstormed the time sequence that would be needed to arrive at school at 8:30 am. Leena would set her own clock for 6:45 am, and it was agreed that for a whole week, neither parent was allowed to knock on the door, or yell or anything: no cajoling, reminding, NOTHING!

With two people in the room rolling their eyes, thinking I was totally the wrong counsellor for their family, I asked, 'Even if this plan is not 100% successful, it wouldn't harm the current school attendance rate which was 0%. So, could each of you please estimate how successful you think this will be? (That is, how many days might Leena get to school next week.) The response was, Mum: 1, Dad: 0 and Leena: 4. I suggested a star

on the calendar may show and celebrate days of Lena's success.

Leena attended two, which was a unique outcome that we unpacked at the next session. Within a month, Leena was attending four out of five days. Leena and her mum came to the last session, sharing the story about school attendance success and Leena made a before and after drawing of her counselling experience.

At least three things worked here:

- finding an alternative name to the problem story created more hope and trust in the family, and less shame
- believing in Leena's capacity to grow and change and acknowledging her ideas
- supporting the parents, but also challenging them about their yelling, without shaming.

They created a family motto 'Never Stop the Love,' and in our last session they created a family Team of Life exercise.

Some people ask me, 'Kim, where do you find all these ideas?' I tell them this story:

Ananse and the Sack of Ideas

At the beginning of time when the world was being created, Ananse the Spiderman came across a sack. He opened it and looked inside. It was full of ideas. It was full of every idea that ever was, or ever would be in the world!

Ananse quickly put that sack over his shoulder and began to climb a tall tree. He was going to find a place to hide these ideas and keep them all for himself.

He climbed and he climbed and he climbed. And just as he neared the top he saw a safe place to tuck that sack away.

But as he lifted the sack from his shoulder, he lost his footing and he could not grip both the sack and a branch to hold himself steady.

The sack opened and the ideas poured out. The Wind rushed by and blew, and blew so hard that the ideas were scattered to every corner of the earth.

And that is why even today, you can come across an idea—anytime and anyplace.

This story was told to Kim Billington by a seven-year-old African girl in a therapeutic storytelling counselling session—in exchange for a story Kim had told her!

Case study: Anxiety

Eight-year-old Patrick had experienced significant trauma over three years, and his presenting problem was 'Anxiety'.

Kim: What does Anxiety feel like?
Patrick: Worries.
Kim: What kind of things do you do when Worries are building up?
Patrick: I like to draw. (Indeed, every time Patrick comes, he has a large sketch book.)
Kim: I know there has been some very difficult things you've experienced, is drawing a shield to keep out The Worries?
Patrick: Well today I made a 'superpower double shield' and I think it's making 'The Annoying Worries' to be 'not as annoying'.
Kim: How is it to talk about these worries, and your holding off The Worries with your shield?
Patrick: Drawing helps me not get 'Shut Down'.
Kim: When does Shut Down and Worries sort of spoil your life?
Patrick: At night-time, just before dinner it starts to ... (Patrick shakes and acts scared.)
I asked Mum and Dad how they might make space for conversations about 'The Worries' at home. We

talked about how the family could gain even more power over the Worry Problem. Patrick chimed in with an idea.

Patrick: I have a few toys who have power and strength: Froakie and Oshawott (Pokémon toys). Patrick said he wanted to invite them to the dinner table to add strength to his shield. His parents agreed, saying they would make sure to create this forcefield.

Kim: Let me know what you intend to call your team, and how well they hold off The Worries.

The next day a photo was emailed to me: 'The Happy Team'. The Pokémon characters stood on the table next to a beaming Patrick! The next week the family phoned to say that Patrick was looking more bright and lighter in his mood.

Two weeks later, Patrick came in and happily declared 'happy at home' was now 9/10 (up from 6/10) and he didn't even need to have everyone from the Happy Team at the table every night.

Toss the coin therapy

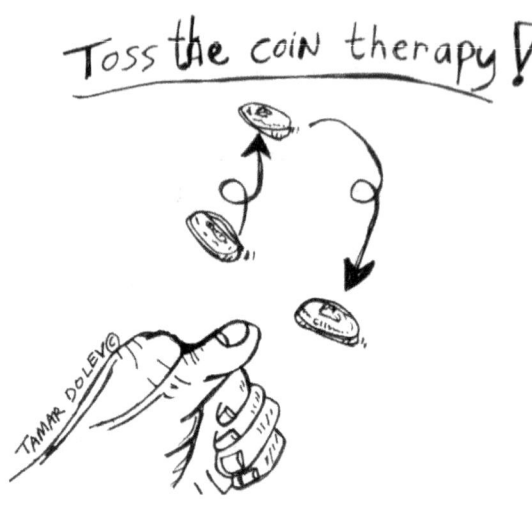

Problems can create such anxiety and self-doubt, that a person may feel unable to make even the smallest of decisions. When called to choose what to do next, I may say that for every 'yes', there must be a 'no'. If you are deciding where to eat out and can't choose between the two, then you must end up saying 'no' to one of them.

Rarely can we have our cake and eat it too. If a teenager wants to end the relationship, but doesn't want to lose the kudos of having a boyfriend and her new social media status, I may discuss intuition, or tell the story of *The Bird in the Cage* (see Chapter 10).

Or, I take another angle. This activity is a problem hack that cuts to the chase. It requires a gut response that guides the person towards their preferred future. I say, 'If plan A (to stay) is heads and plan B (to go) is tails, as the coin twirls in the air, what do you hope it lands on?' I then toss an imaginary coin (because who has coins in the 21st century?).

When they answer, I can ask what three things helped them choose that preferred direction?

'Your heart knows the way.
Run in that direction.'
Rumi

Summary

Hacking The Problem using externalising metaphors creates new perspectives and fresh ideas can spring to life. We can track small shifts in the balance of power, as the child's new story and actions outgrow The Problem's dull, old story. In counselling, confidence and courage gather around, and a cascade of new possibilities becomes visible.

Believing in the child's imaginative, solution capacities helps them believe in themselves. What they say matters. Their voice is heard, and we take them seriously, but in a playful way. Taking back some power from the problem is the way we play the narrative therapy game.

> *'Believe you can and you're halfway there.'*
> **Theodore Roosevelt**

Actions to take as a result of reading this chapter

1. Make a decision to work on one small problem that has been bothering you. Try and hack it. Write down why it bothers you? When is it not such a bother? Scale its presence in your day. Use your imagination to see a way forward. What metaphor may suit? How will you take action? How will you celebrate your success?

2. Explore the latest research about anxiety. Start with Dr Gabor Maté.

3. Check out David Epston's website for more creative narrative approaches: (http://www.narrativeapproaches.com/tag/anti-anorexia/).

CHAPTER 5

Roller-Coaster of Emotions

'Colours, like features, follow the changes of the emotions.'

PABLO PICASSO

Who isn't looking for comfort, calm, joy, safety, hope, connection, love and purpose? Every child has some memories of happy moments—can you remember some of yours?

Emotions are never 'bad' or 'negative'. Emotions come and go. When they arrive, we sense them in subtle, or strong bodily pressures. They are part of our ancient, internal alert system that says, 'Okay, something needs your attention. Please check it out'.

Children can be overwhelmed by uncomfortable emotions, and the effects of trauma impacts their ability to feel happy, play freely, make stable social connections, and focus in a learning environment. This chapter includes approaches to assist with post-trauma recovery.

Children as young as two will soon learn to protect themselves and avoid the uncomfortable, social emotion of shame by telling a lie. Perhaps they pushed another child or took that extra cookie. They soon learn ways to avoid feeling shame or bearing the wrath of their parent.

Every emotion is part of life and has survival purposes. They arrive in our bodies as tight sensations/sweating/knee knocking, etc. We learn to interpret these, and may express them as feelings, verbally, such as 'I'm scared of going to school' or respond to them by curling up.

Helping Parents

Having responsibility for a child can stir up some forgotten, silent rage, as Seigel and Hartzell, point out in their book *Parenting from the Inside Out*. However, children are watching and learning and imitate what they have seen.

Most parents intend to be kind and responsive, yet soon stumble into repeating parental behaviour patterns they may have been subject to themselves as a child. Our own unresolved childhood emotions may be sitting in the centre of the tiniest of the babushka dolls.

I have a fireman babushka doll and I use these to remind older children and adults that our well contained, supressed childhood (and later) experiences are all still there, and children can be sensitive to being around those with long supressed emotions. I developed the doll as a symbol in therapy after reading Bessel van der Kolk's book *The Body Keeps the Score*.

I may say, 'Outside you look like a grown up parent, but inside everyone is their smaller self and it is always communicating with us. Nobody I've ever met has had parents that anticipated, and met their every need. So there would have been times when you also felt unhappy or let down by your own parents'.

As a counsellor, we too can realise those emotions are still there in us. We may become unsettled when our clients express strong emotions, because this vibration resonates and takes us back to a time when we were feeling powerless and angry. The tiniest doll reminds us that everyone we meet has unmet needs from when they were little.

A practice I do to explore this is based on the Compassion Focused Therapy approach developed by Paul Gilbert and Russell Kolts. I make time to sit quietly, with hands on belly and heart. The layers of all my experiences are still available to me. I can revisit the emotions and practise re-parenting myself with compassion.

My self-talk goes like this: 'Notice where you are feeling this now. Listen to that little crying self. *I can hear you. It's okay, I am here now for you.*'

In 1999, the *Tuning In To Kids* parenting program arrived. It was a revolutionary, evidence-based and neurologically informed approach to show parents different ways to respond to strong emotions. In 2015, the Pixar children's film, *Inside Out* was a watershed moment for many parents, because it externalised the five core emotions in an entertaining way. This enabled people to talk about some challenging big feelings: Fear, Anger, Joy, Disgust and Sadness.

With children

Having a language to name feelings and know when we are in The Red Zone territory might be helpful knowledge to a child.

Windows of Tolerance

Panic
Anger
Scared — The Red Zone

Worried
O.K
This is my GReeN O.K ZoNe
Sad
Disappointed
Hurt

The BLue Zone

Grief
Ashamed
Despair

TAMAR©

As an alternative to Dan Siegel's Windows of Tolerance model, I designed a snakes and ladder image using the vibrational energy model of emotions. 'How do you lift yourself up? Why is that choice important to you?' Young people can design and colour their own version to increase awareness and communication around emotional states.

Usually, it is our responses to emotions that might be unhelpful. If children can be taught to lean into the emotion, they will not fear or be ashamed of them, but notice, recognise and even welcome them.

I may ask a child to notice where in the body is the energy of the emotion. They don't have to find feeling words. They can simply place their hands on their heart/belly and apply a slight pressure to offer comfort, then take three breaths: in slowly through the nose, and out slowly through slightly parted lips.

With older children, you may be interested in trying Daniel Siegel's SIFT technique, from his book *The Whole Brain Child*, by asking, 'What are your sensations, images, feelings and thoughts?'

I convey the importance of crying as an emotional release. Research shows that crying forces the body to slow down its breathing, and the self-soothing effects of crying activates the parasympathetic nervous system and increases oxytocin. After this, there can be a fresh reappraisal of an experience. The chemical composition of onion-slicing tears are different from emotion tears. Crying with an emotional release triggers a natural painkiller, leucine enkephalin and also relieves our body of stress hormones.

I sometimes tell my adult and child clients therapeutic stories. Like a metaphor, folktales engage the part of the brain that can put aside the analytical, black and white thinking, and open up new possibilities for making sense of our lives (see Chapter 8). They bring the body to a quiet state. A story I often share is a folktale from China, *The Empty Pot*. It tells the story of an old emperor who is looking for an heir to his throne, and his clever plan to find an honest and trustworthy successor. Like many other classic tales, the simple story about Yun and the empty pot evokes many emotions that encourage self-reflection and discussion.

Ref: https://storiestogrowby.org/story/empty-pot/

Creative interventions to increase emotional awareness

There are many emotional regulation and creative art therapies that are grounding and can slow down the heart rate. These activities can lead to restoring safety, re-establishing connection and belonging, and reconstitute and renew identity. The simple act of choosing which colour to paint with, begins a healing journey.

Here are a few of my favourite playful, expressive art activities for children:

1. Drawing a spiral: On the whiteboard or paper, begin at the edge, and slowly, slowly take a minute to come to the centre without lifting the pencil. I often do this alongside the child, at the beginning of a session. At the end of the session, on a new piece of paper, we draw another spiral beginning at the centre, and slowly moving outwards to the edge.

This exercise is both mindful and is a wonderful assessment of how the child is travelling. Each of the two parts works quite differently. With adolescents, I extend these using Jon Harris' instructional YouTube videos such as Spiral Drawing #388, Practice Curves 3D Pattern, Satisfying Line Illusion and Daily Art Therapy.

2. Masked feelings: Everyone wears a mask. Is it a lie to do that? Why do we choose to do this? Might we be simply copying a parent? When is it helpful to wear a mask? When might it not be helpful?

With young children, they can draw their body with the face they usually put on when they go outside the house. They may also draw a picture of how they look when at home, school, basketball, Grandma's, etc. With older children, I guide them through the T-shirt exercise. They draw a T-shirt on one side of the paper, and another on the back. The 'front' is labelled and on that T-shirt they write down all the feelings they are happy to express to others (guided by an emotion wheel downloaded from the internet). On the back, they write down the feelings and thoughts they hide from others.

3. Family sculpting: This is an extension of free expression using clay, which can sometimes include throwing the clay onto the table and pounding it with fists. Here, the child is invited to use the clay to sculpt some friends or family members, including themselves and pets. This is similar to the animal genogram, where plastic animals and symbols can be placed in relationship to each other to show their preferred proximity to each family member. I have found this works well in combination with The Bears Cards.

4. Painting: This can be on paper, or outside using cardboard in mural style. This is often an expression of big emotions that have been kept in, so watch out! Wear aprons and cover any carpet. Finger painting tends to resonate with emotions of joy, celebration and happiness. A 10-year-old boy who had to move houses several times due to family violence, said he wanted to be a builder when he grew up, so they can all live in their own house. I brought in a big box, and over several sessions, he cut out windows and doors and painted the house he built, then took it home.

5. Role-play: Many children think they won't like this when I suggest it, but it gets them up out of their chair, and with movement plus a scene and plot, they can step into character quite well. This can be preparation for a part-time job interview, responding to a new step-parent, or how it feels to express anger assertively, passively or nastily. It can be how they wish they had acted, or it can be mimed for a release of stress, or a preferred future encounter.

I ask the child to take a few seconds to get in-role, which means come out of your head, into the body and be prepared to allow a powerful emotion to be felt in a safe space. We can swap roles and repeat a few times then talk about how that felt. It doesn't mean this will give the child the confidence to actually follow through! It is simply playing with ideas and ways to express and move our emotions. Coming out of the role afterwards, by bringing the child's attention to sounds in the room may be necessary for some of the more intense ones.

6. Vision board: Using cut out magazines or images printed from the internet, the child chooses a backing coloured piece of paper and arranges words and pictures to represent either what they hope for the future or what they have been enjoying now. This is usually a celebratory experience.

It works really well as a parent-child last session activity. I usually play some gentle music and leave the room for 10 minutes to allow for some quality bonding times as they chat and search for images the other might like. A father-son exercise was one of my most memorable vision board activities. I returned to the room, and Dad's page had a glass of beer, a sports car and gym equipment. He said, 'When you first left us in the room with this basket of magazines, I thought this is just crazy. But I've really found it to be helpful. I've been close with my son, and it's given me time to be in this quiet zone, I've not been in before. Thank you'.

7. Sand tray: This can provide the child with an opportunity to tell their story using symbols placed in the sand. Through telling their story in this way, the child has the opportunity to non-verbally recreate experiences from the past, how things are now and explore future possibilities.

8. What anxiety looks like: Using collage craft materials, and alternative words from the thesaurus, I invite the child to creatively express the anxiety that they know, in any way they like. The textures and kinaesthetic activity can be very calming. Another well-known activity is to create a 'glitter jar' to demonstrate a stirred-up, anxious state becoming calm over time. Instructions for this can be found on YouTube.

9. Drawing something that scares you: If a child has had a serious trauma and I'm not sure what to do next, I suggest they can draw something on a piece of paper to represent the terrible things or even horrible dreams, or their feelings about the terrible things. Then they can then shred, tear-up, scrunch, jump on, cut up with scissors, or in any way show that they were NOT happy

with that happening to them. I show them the DANGER BOX I keep in my care, and say that this box is full to the brim with just such stories and I let them peek inside, but quickly put the lid back on and tie it up with the black ribbon.

10. Cat moods: Let's sit like a cat, quietly alert and paws folded. Then we can pose as cats having quite different feelings (These may be written on paper in a decorated cat box):
Scared: get down, ears back, hiss, growl, or run away and hide.
Happy: calm, raised curving tail, soft eyes with slow blinks, and a gentle purr.
Worried: bite or scratch, can't stay still.
Annoyed: fast wagging tail, loud and long vocalisations, swat with the paw.
Aggressive: growl, lunge and swat with a stiff body with erect hackles, bared teeth and ears pulled back.
Hungry: very vocal with short, high-pitched meows.
Affectionate: head bunting, social grooming, slow eye blinks, purring and choosing to sit next to you, but maybe with their back to you, which is a display of trust.

11. Snappy dog: This game needs some time creating a deck of cards. But I have found it to be THE best emotion conversation game. I use it all the time, even online, I can tilt the camera down and turn the cards over one at a time. Search 'Google + Image: dog + emotion + feelings' then choose and save about eight different emotional expressions on dogs (jealousy, scared, etc.). Crop to a slightly larger than playing card size. Print 8 copies of each on sturdy paper. Cut the corners, so they are rounded and begin the game. It plays like regular snap, and when a double is seen, any player can call out 'snap!'. Then they have to (1) name what they think the dog's emotion is, and (2) tell a short story of when they last had that same emotion.

Grounding and mindfulness

There are many techniques such as progressive muscle relaxation and body scans, where we invite a child or young person to connect with themselves. These may be contraindicative if a child has recently experienced trauma or is in a heightened state. Rocking, gently bouncing on a trampoline or other vestibular activities may be more suitable in this case.

With primary school aged children, we may watch and talk about a four-minute video, 'Just Breathe'. The children in the film talk about slowing down and noticing their breath. It was created by Mindful Schools graduate and filmmaker, Julie Bayer Salzman (YouTube: https://youtu.be/RVA2N6tX2cg)

I use the following guided imagery for children aged 10 years upwards, to invite them to create their own images. It takes about four minutes and allows us to hear more about the 'moment in time' they imagined. Later they might like to draw, or create a scene using clay or sand. Many have found it helpful to prepare the body and mind for sleep.

Finding a precious place, and a moment in time

- You have arrived at a place where you can take a holiday. You are free from the usual demands in this moment of time.
- The little house where you are to stay has a lovely view. You look around, and then decide to go for a walk. You breathe in ... and out ... The fresh air fills your lungs. Life and goodness fill your whole body.

- The fresh grass looks so inviting, you decide to take off your shoes, and walk with your bare feet touching the earth. Every step is soft and comfortable.
- As you look around, you see a rock in the shade of a tree that invites you to sit down.
- As you sit there, the strong, stillness of the rock feels welcoming. This is the right time and the right place to be here.
- In this place you can completely relax. In this moment in time, you can simply be.
- A beautiful animal appears nearby. You watch its graceful movements, and feel connected to nature. It passes by, and you look up to see the sky above.
- What else can you see as you look around? Describe it in your mind, noticing each beautiful detail.
- Pay attention to what you can hear.
- What other senses are sharing their experience with you? Is there warmth, a light breeze?
- When you are ready, give your moment in time a name … a title.
- And when you are ready, have one last and slow look around, taking it all in.
- And now you are ready, slowly fold-up your moment in time, and put it in your pocket.
- Come back to your chair … taking a slow, deep, in-breath, stretch your arms slowly, and let out the breath, through the mouth, with a big sigh … haaaaaaaaa.

Case study: Fear of failure

Abe is a 17-year-old struggling to stay focused in his final year at school. He is experiencing fears of failure due to lost motivation and missed assignments. Fear was the presenting issue. We soon concluded that Anxiety was teaming up with Fears and School Pressure, creating very little space for Abe to chill out and enjoy his close circle of friends.

Looking back at May, and projecting forwards to November and January, Abe scored his struggles. He saw that numerically he believed things would improve. This gave him hope.

"Exploring Fears into the Future" 17 years old

Fears	May	Aug	Nov	Jan
Anxiety	6/10	8/10	8½/10	4/10
School Pressure	7/10	9/10	6/10	1/10

TAMAR DOLEV©

He also searched 'Google + quote + fear' and chose this from Jack Canfield: *'Everything you want is on the other side of fear.'*

I asked Abe, 'What would it mean if the Fear was not as annoying or big, and how is the problem influencing your plans for the future?'. Abe said he'd be walking into final exams more chilled if Fear was less, and if he couldn't turn this around he would flunk.

Abe said he went to a place with no fear as he was listening to me share the 'Finding a precious place, and a moment in time' visualisation. Some bullying in the previous year was identified as we explored the history of the problem. Abe thought he may have some 'small-t' trauma, as he beautifully described it. He became curious and engaged with psych-ed around how he had responded to fear in the past, saying that 'staying in the freeze zone' was his pattern now too. It was disconnecting him from his dreams. Abe used the hand-on-heart/belly grounding when The Fear arrived, and found a new confidence that he could be influential over these intense feelings.

Questions I used to explore the effects of Fears included 'Why is having Fear not such a good thing? What does Fear have you thinking about yourself? What might you say back to Fear?'

I told Abe the American Indian story about Two Wolves (shown in Chapter 8) and asked him, 'How might you starve your problem and feed your solution?'.

Working on Fears enabled Abe to gain ground from Anxiety by using hope, self-talk and mindfulness.

Abe then spoke about some stress in his renewed relationship with his father. Before Abe was born, his mum left his father due to his alcohol problems. Abe had begun seeing his dad for a few hours each month recently. Using an emotion wheel, Abe identified sadness, rejection and shame as the three main emotions he could not 'shake-off' from his 'difficult childhood *without* a father'. Mum had never re-partnered. Abe admitted she was amazing, but said he was now feeling rage towards her about his 'messed-up childhood'. These mixed feelings left him confused.

I asked Abe if he could draw a three generational, cartoon-style story of his life.

The picture revealed his own father probably struggled in a 'difficult childhood *with* a father'. Abe's grandfather had been an overbearing and violent man. We postulated that Abe's father may have even experienced the same emotions as

Abe: sadness, rejection and shame. This parallel was a turning point for Abe.

It led to some existential discussions about life and how he might use freedom to create the path he wanted as a man, and as a future dad. I introduced Abe to Russel Kolts' YouTube video about Anger and Compassion Focussed Therapy which he found stimulating. This empowered him to move forwards and 'shake-off' some of the hurts he'd been holding on to.

By drawing and reflecting on his story, Abe's problems were further externalised and he made space for new meanings. He became curious and excited about how he might write his own next chapter.

Summary

Emotions play a large role in how humans respond to one another. Knowing how to identify and deal with strong emotions can help people have happier relationships. It can help to remember that emotions can be culturally and socially constrained, according to gender, age, status, etc. although young children initially express everything, without guard.

Emotional intelligence continues to develop throughout life. We can foster in children a freedom to express emotions in ways that do not harm others.

Actions to take as a result of reading this chapter

1. Choose a child-friendly 'feelings faces' poster and an emotion wheel online or in print.

2. Enrol in a *Tuning In To Kids/Tuning In To Teens* course to skill-up on emotion coaching using John Gottman's work.

3. Become more mindful of changes in your emotional body. Place your hand with firm pressure where there is any tension/energy, and breathe. Practise CFT: Compassion Focused Therapy 're-parenting' self-talk.

CHAPTER 6

The Fork in the Road

'Where there is anger there is always pain underneath.'
ECKHART TOLLE

The history of the problem is always a helpful line of enquiry, but with anger we may need to act swiftly to support the person to find new ways to ensure harm to others is reduced.

If a child has been walking down the road with a Tiger Tantrum shadowing them, the shame and guilt may blind them to alternative routes. I often speak about the fork in the road, saying 'You're at a crossroads now. Life has said, "Stop here. Choose what direction you want your life to be going in"'. Older children can be asked for their thoughts about Aristotle's awareness of the challenges around taming that tiger, written more than 2000 years ago:

> *'Anybody can become angry, that is easy; but to be angry with the right person, and to the right degree, and at the right time, and for the right purpose, and in the right way, that is not within everybody's power, that is not easy.'*
>
> **Aristotle, in his classic work *The Art of Rhetoric***

With curiosity and non-judgement I am always pleased when the child/parent displays anger during a session. I can say, 'Wow, so is this the kind of Tiger Temper that explodes at home? Is Home Anger bigger or smaller than this one?'

Case study: The fork in the road

Eleven-year-old Jack arrives with his mum and dad. Mum had told me in the phone intake that she and Jack get on really well, but Jack has been mistreating his younger siblings, and was defiant, especially with Dad. When I asked what they'd tried, she said, 'I'm getting Jack to write in a gratitude journal each night, because he has so much to be grateful for. But it's not helping him get less angry. He and his dad are having terrible arguments'.

At the end of the session I said to the parents, 'I want to ask Jack a question, and I'd like you to support his answer, are you okay with that?' Mum and Dad hesitated, looked at each other then said it was okay.

I turned to Jack and said, 'You know Jack, anger problems are not that hard to deal with. Now you've met me, are you prepared to come back here to meet me on your own a couple of times, and sometimes with a parent. Can you choose either just Mum, or just Dad?' Jack said yes, and after a quick glance at them both, said, 'Dad'.

In the second session I heard more about who Jack is, as well as the problem story. I introduced the 'fork in the road' metaphor. Jack googled lots of danger images, warning signs and even an actual fork in the road! We printed these, and he cut and glued them onto some cardboard. He had an image of himself carrying a suitcase full of all the bottled-up feelings he identified: sadness, worry, frustration and resentment.

We discussed where the anger road was heading ... loss of privileges and losing his good times with Dad. The sign he chose at the end of that road was, 'Steep Cliff'.

Then Jack got excited about the fact he had a choice, and his big takeaway was that he wanted his family to cheer him on with his efforts to manage his temper. He wanted them to celebrate his successes. He proudly took the picture home, and put a copy on the counselling room wall for other children to see.

In the weeks that followed, we had three father-son sessions. They were some of the most tender and memorable in my practice. Dad took responsibility for his own mean ways and his serious anger problem. He said he had been blaming Jack for his own anger, which he thought was coming out when he saw Jack being cruel to the younger siblings.

This brave father told Jack and I that his own older brother, Uncle Pete had been a bully to him when he was growing up. Dad said he had always felt ashamed. He still had all this pent-up anger, and now was being the bully. There were hugs and tears, and high-fives.

They decided to take home some star stickers to put on the kitchen calendar when they'd both achieved a full day of refusing the invitations of Anger, and this worked for them. (I am not usually a fan of reward charts, but this collaborative goal seemed to be a perfect fit.)

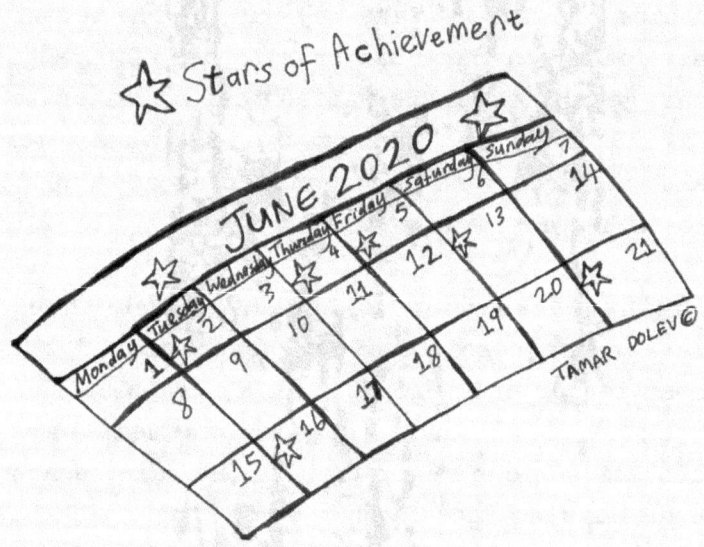

They finished the last session together doing a vision board each. (See Chapter 5) Dad's images cut-out from magazines included a beer glass and a gym set. Jack's had a sporting theme. The counselling had come at the perfect time just before Jack hit adolescence. Dad saw that he needed more help himself, and booked to see a male psychologist.

What is anger?

Once we understand some of the universal mechanisms of anger, we can therapeutically embrace it. People usually escalate to a visible, and often intimidating expression of anger once a value or boundary they've set is breached. They may fall back into shame and sadness, but out of powerlessness a rage can simmer again, triggering guilt and confusion.

Then we may indeed see how DANGER is just one letter ahead of ANGER.

If a child's favourite toy is broken by another child, or they are not allowed to watch a movie they'd been looking forward to, feelings of indignation and resentment can explode like a volcano. I ask, 'What three emotions are happening just before anger erupts?'

Children know exactly what anger looks like, because it is a form of communication that demands to be heard and seen. My first narrative therapy lecturer, Ron Findlay, spoke to us about considering anger as a 'secondary emotion,' that can be used as an 'act' of status restoration. This concept has been very helpful in my work when 'anger management issues' is written on the intake form.

How might we help children, and parents, befriend anger? Is there a practice that can be introduced when times are calm, that will rewire the brain and bring a preparedness for the inevitable next episode?

Firstly, children must know we were not designed for 24/7 calm. There will be emotional storms emerging and subsiding.

Here are two guiding questions:
Can you notice when a storm is brewing?
Can you prepare yourself to receive the storm, and handle it when it arrives?

Mindful responses

I have developed a guided grounding commentary combining ideas from both the Rock and Water program, and Thich Nhat Hanh's Zen practices:

> *Breathe in through your nose, deep into your belly, and exhale—three times. You are like a tall tree. In a storm, your topmost branches will be tossed from side to side, but the trunk will be firm. You have deep roots going down into the earth. Bring your awareness to your belly.*
>
> *Emotions are an energy, and mindfulness is a kind of energy too. Mindfulness is a superpower that is strong and kind. It notices every emotion, and can calm the storm. Embrace your anger like a mother, saying, 'Hello my little anger, I know that you are there. I will take good care of you. I am smiling at you. I am not going to run away from you. I am standing strong beside you. I have noticed you, and in my arms I am holding you'.*
>
> *Emotions seem to rise, and want to take hold, but we know they will pass. Say to yourself, 'I have survived these emotions before, and I can survive the ones that will arrive again in the future. Emotions come and go. I am more than an emotion'.*

Each time you get through a strong emotion, that is an achievement.

Working with parents

I discuss anger with parents using this simple anecdote: When another driver cuts in front of you, dangerously close just before the lights ... the first emotion, without any thought process required, is fear. This is accompanied by an instinctive slamming on the brakes. Only then does the fear turn to a conscious act of anger: the horn is honked, and expletives are let out in an attempt to remedy the powerlessness that they made you feel.

Anger is often about attempts to reclaim a loss of power through a show of force. I may ask a parent, 'When your child is heading towards an explosion into anger, can you pause and consider *what might my child need?*' Connection before correction is a motto for parents, and comes from the *Tuning in to Kids* training I completed 20 years ago.

I am a believer that nobody can 'make me angry'. It's a choice, every time who we show our anger to.

> *'Do not teach your children never to be angry;*
> *teach them how to be angry.'*
> **Lyman Abbott**

Even very young people calculate the risks of unleashing anger, and in freedom, perform acts of anger, driven by unacknowledged frustrations. An example is how a child may hit one parent but not the other. Children can be introduced to the ideas around taking responsibility for the effects of anger on others. This can hopefully reduce the likelihood of them being tricked into repeating harmful patterns from their parents, or creating relationships in the future where they seek power and control.

I've found that counsellors who've been exposed to excessive anger or violence in their own childhoods can still be living with remnants of fear, deep inside that babushka doll. They may be adversely affected by some of their cases, and so may benefit from additional support. The next case study is tagged with a trigger warning.

Case study: Snake learns to hiss

Nine-year-old Daniel was having his first month ever without being subjected to violence. For his whole life, he could never express his fury to his own father, whose violence had been at a dangerous level since before Daniel's birth. After 10 years of horrific abuse, the mother gained an intervention order and fled with her son.

The referral came to the family violence agency because social workers at the refuge had seen Daniel self-harming. He was on a waiting list for a psychiatric assessment. He was clearly struggling with many symptoms of post-traumatic stress, which included fears at night, and bursts of anger.

At the end of our first session, I asked Daniel, 'Would you like me to tell you a story next week? You can choose the topic'. Daniel straightaway asked for a story about a snake. I looked online and found *How the Snake Got Poison*, an African

American folktale retold by Zora Neale Hurston, which I hoped would resonate with him. It is about a powerless snake who felt he was treated unfairly by God, because he had no legs and no protection from his enemies. He complained to God, and was given poison, but soon the other animals were unhappy that Snake was using his poison too freely. God then gave Snake a hiss and bells on his tail which he could use as a warning to protect himself, rather than using his poison every time he felt threatened.

The next session, Daniel arrived looking relaxed unlike his unease in the first meeting. He sat expectantly for his story and listened intensely. He said the snake was very brave to go and complain. Daniel then drew a picture of Snake hiding in a bush, with a giant, messy black monster animal looming over.

The next week, I asked a question to gather any meanings he was forming from the snake story. 'In what ways did you relate to the journey of the hero?' Daniel said it reminded him that he could not run away when they were at the old home (where his father was still living now). He said he was pleased I had chosen a snake story, as he had asked.

Daniel then declared he had a story for me, and on the spot created a story about a spider, who did not have all of his eight legs. 'The mother spider was very embarrassed, but she prayed and prayed. At last one morning the spider noticed that he'd grown the eighth leg, and everything would be okay.' I wrote down his story and he illustrated it.

In the recent weeks of chaos and fears leading up to the night of the great escape from the violent family home, Daniel had been scratching his arms and legs with his fingernails, so that welts had formed. I decided to use his love of stories to introduce my understanding of his trauma.

Supporting children who have begun to harm their bodies is now a part of most clinician's work. For some children, this act may be the one thing they have control over in their response to unimaginable stress and limited personal agency. I believe it's important to speak quite frankly about self-harm, asking such questions as 'How different is Stress this week, higher, the same, or lower? How often have you turned to cutting to cope? Do you have any new thoughts of ending your life? How else might you prefer to respond to this pain?' With Daniel being so young, I began with more tentativeness, and used the metaphor of a novel.

I asked Daniel if he could see that the first difficult chapter of his life has now ended, and now he was safely living with Mum at the refuge. The trauma work with Daniel included something important I learnt from Babette Rothschild in her book *8 Keys to Safe Trauma Recovery*: that we need to help our clients realise that the trauma has ended.

The book metaphor externalised his first traumatic nine years. He was being invited to adapt to what had happened, which would be a lifetime task. He and his mum had survived to write their own future chapters. Over several weekly sessions, Daniel used the Strengths Cards®, The Bears cards and the Kimochis® feelings chart to show and talk about how he got through those hard times.

I shared my Bag of Walnuts story (see Chapter 10) and afterwards, Daniel said that his life was also not fair. I talk to all my clients about what is a 'normal' response when something not okay and unfair happens to them. How when your safety and wellbeing has been violated, rage of indignation and righteous anger can erupt, which is a totally understandable response.

We looked at the fight-flight-freeze cartoon images (see page 163) and I said aloud that I wondered if maybe the scratching was a way of him connecting to that anger? This interested Daniel and we found a metaphor in a protective tiger mother to demonstrate this. This conversation was pivotal. Daniel saw his recent Tiger Tantrums and scratching made sense. Daniel said he was the kind of Tiger who could take responsibility for his new power and take care not to hurt others or himself.

I introduced a simple, half-minute technique that can reduce stress, which I use in online counselling where a more lengthy grounding, body scan may feel too imposing. The young person breathes in through their nose as they lift their arms slowly above the head. Hold for the count of two, then slowly lower the arms, breathing out through a slightly parted mouth, making a phooo sound. Once is usually enough. I avoid the words relax or calm, preferring to enquire about the efficacy of anything I do later.

I returned to the book metaphor, and told Daniel I was picturing how the first chapter of his life story had now ended, and that as I turned the page, I could see the birth of a new beginning, and asked him if that was an image he could see too, and might this help him.

Over the coming weeks, we told more stories, and Daniel made clay snakes and a diorama for them. They were all sizes and were looking safe, as there were no enemies around. I asked the refuge staff to buy some clay for him, and Daniel and Mum reported the scratching stopped.

A month later, Daniel and his mum relocated interstate. Although he would require further support in the years ahead, he had an opportunity to be given choices and exercise some control, by choosing which stories I would tell each week. He found a way to make sense of his self-harm. I gave him the Christopher Reeve quote:

'There will be many chapters in your life. Don't get lost in the one you're in now.'

By using the book chapter metaphor as a re-authoring tool, Daniel found a normalising way to refer to those dark years. Daniel recognised he'd been powerless and hurt in his first life story chapter, and that his emotions were based on what he had experienced. The chapter headings externalised the old problem, and the new directions. Daniel found a way to gather hopes for the future. The clay snakes slithering freely in safety were an image of that.

Responding to trauma

No client is a passive recipient of abuse. One 19-year-old said she used to pull faces as soon as the perpetrator, an older cousin, turned and was leaving her bedroom. She had told me, 'I'm so ashamed I never told anyone and stopped him. He did it to others I'm sure. I knew it was something wrong, but I didn't even know what it was back then'. The case was already in court. Sharing the small things she did to safely demonstrate her fury, and other things to protect herself against the abuse, reminded her that she did what she could at the time as a little child (see Appendix 1 for responding to risk).

Reflection

Such challenging cases can be emotionally exhausting for clinicians, with many suffering from compassion fatigue. However, I have found narrative therapy can help me survive and thrive in this intense work, with its useful creative approaches and invitational, re-authoring questions.

I can write these case studies now, in what seems to be a dispassionate way, but you may be sure I have received excellent and regular supervision over the years. I take this opportunity now, to acknowledge Cheryl Taylor and Vivienne Mountain who have walked beside me on my journey from novice counsellor, to counselling supervisor. I am deeply grateful to you both for your warm and wise supervision, support and encouragement.

In addition, I have always made sure that each week includes quality 'Kim Time': meaningful self-care practices for my body and soul. I recognise the signs when burnout is creeping close, and I book another supervision session or a 90-minute massage.

Summary

Anger is a choice. It is something we enact after a disappointment, or when our boundaries have been violated. Anger can be used to maintain power over others, or to attempt to gain back some power and influence. Understanding the history of this problem often leads to hearing about parental rage in response to their own powerless and traumatic childhoods.

Anger can be a catalyst for change. When parents see their child is acting in ways they're worried about, and come to counselling, all the family can find some new meaning, relief and move towards recovery.

Actions to take as a result of reading this chapter

1. Consider registering for the Australian Childhood Foundation's biannual International Childhood Trauma Conference for access to many valuable resources including masterclasses, keynote presentations, networking and more.

2. Visit my website and download the colourful drawing of The Geology of Anger.

3. Investigate mindfulness for emotional awareness and regulation. For example, read a book from the Buddhist perspective, and one from neuroscience such as Daniel Siegel's *The Mindful Brain*, or watch a Kristin Neff YouTube.

CHAPTER 7

The Unfairness of Loss

'There is no normative blueprint for grieving.'
GLENDA FREDMAN

Children need freedom and safety to talk about missing someone who has died or gone away. Their feelings may come and go, so parents may not be sure if their child's grief is becoming a serious problem.

When Loss arrives, it can feel unfair and isolating, since others may not understand or have experienced such a loss. With counselling support, children can begin to make sense of a new life after the loss.

'Sometimes two homes are better than one.'
Nine-year-old after family separation

'Mummy is looking after Tinkerbell now.'
**Seven-year-old after mother's death,
the month after their cat died**

Many children choose an emoji or Bear Card for sadness when first asked about feelings, so I usually ask, 'What three feelings are happening for you?'. Sadness typically arrives first, with Confusion and Anger often arriving later. Children also feel profound loss around parental separation, since the family home represents safety, and the parents themselves might not be as emotionally available as they are struggling too.

As counsellors, we need to have therapeutic skills and fortitude to help us feel less overwhelmed when troubling referrals arrive, and we see children suffer a significant loss, or as parents battle for financial and so-called 'custodial' powers.

Case study: Dad has left home

Following his mum and dad's separation due to family violence, four-year-old James had been having violent angry outbursts and then crying for a long time, becoming emotionally exhausted. His two-year-old brother matter-of-factly said, 'Dad has left home'.

James came for his first visit and really liked a picture another child had drawn about being 'mad and sad'. I asked if he would like to draw a picture. I offered my big box of stickers and said these may help. He was delighted to select some emojis and dogs and drew a house with four rooms. Each room in his house held a feeling. This was an externalised image of his experience. He asked me to write some words on the whiteboard, which he valiantly copied.

James seemed more settled after finishing and told stories about what had happened at home with Dad, and how he was feeling about each room except the sad room. He stood quietly and when I looked closely, I saw his self-image was standing in the sad room. There was a flooding of tears in the picture. I said, 'This little boy in the sad room has been crying a lot of tears'. James said, 'My family is broken now'. I asked, 'Would you like to share your picture on the wall, if you think it might help other children just like you?'

I was able to see James many times after this, and he was always proud and pleased when I would let him know that nearly every child would stand before James' picture and say 'Yes, that's how it is'. James particularly enjoyed using a tyrannosaurus puppet, he called the Mad Monster to break down a cardboard box house he built in session. Each week, he got his damaged house from behind the sofa. We repaired it with masking tape, for it to endure another hurricane of fury.

In my work in a family mediation centre, the post-separation counselling was non-stop. I developed a template of two houses to help children who were not keen to draw. They simply could add in the people. I had the words, 'My Family' written top centre (see image on page 6). There was a road joining the two houses, and children liked to draw their parent's cars on it and talk about the ups and downs of their post-separation experience. They would add pets, and many used stormy weather, or only a tiny amount of sunshine to express the mood.

What is grief?

When we lose someone or something important to us, our body will change energetically. We can use our hand to connect with this energy and breathe into any inner discomfort. Compassion focused therapy can help direct our approach to working with children. I ask children to ask their kinder, wiser self to whisper gentle and encouraging words we would use to comfort a friend in need.

I usually model what this self-talk looks like, with hands on heart and belly. I ask the child or young person to follow me, but using their own name:

'It's okay, (Kim) we will get through this. I'm here for you. Take a deep breath, and let it out slowly.'

When the realisation that things will never be the same again arrives, denial or disbelief are put to one side for a while, until they return again. Denial is another way of saying, 'I don't want this to be real'. Then feelings of emptiness, guilt, blame or anger towards another arise, in no particular order.

I have found an image that has helped many young people make sense of any loss. I first found it online by searching 'Google + Image + hurdles of grief' and have adapted it from a Kübler-Ross stages theory (which is generally no longer used). I may say, 'Sometimes you can find yourself back to the start, just like in a snakes and ladders game. It's okay to fall apart again and again. Tears release the (cortisol) stress hormones and so let them flow. As you pick yourself up, know that there will be people around you who you can reach out to'.

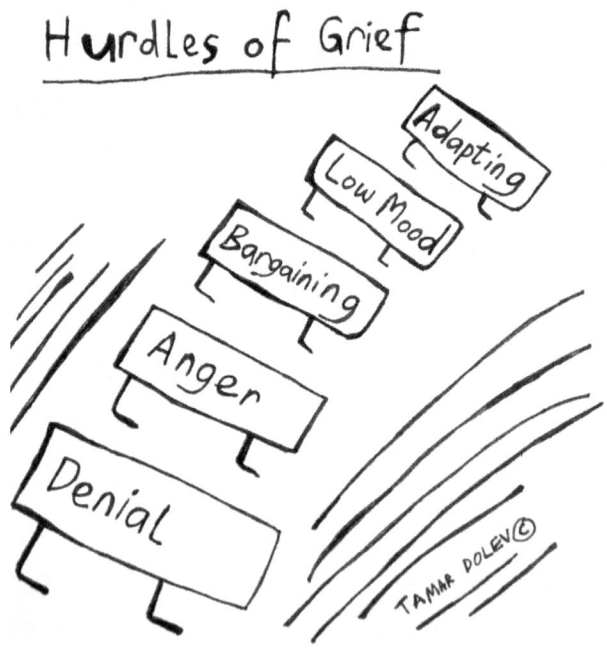

There is no right or wrong way to feel, because just as people display joy or excitement in their own way, everyone grieves in their own way too. There is no set sequence or timetable. 'The size of your grief and tears are equal to the love and connection with (the person/pet/dream).'

I may remind the family that grief comes in waves. Could they each find a metaphor and draw a picture or use colours to show where they are now. A PDF tool of a grief journey is available on my website. It uses pictures of a boat setting out from harbour, encountering a storm, another boat coming to their aid with supplies, and the return. These all follow what Joseph Campbell calls 'The Hero's Journey' (see Chapter 8).

There used to be an attitude last century that you must learn to 'let go'. This is no longer recommended, either in the words, or sentiment. If anything, we now encourage people to find their own ways to stay connected.

With one family, I suggested to the father that he drapes Mum's cardigan over a kitchen chair. Dad put little things in her pockets for the children. On special 'memorial' days there was a note or a treat (like a Christmas stocking).

Case study: Mum hasn't gone far

Sharon is a 69-year-old grandmother who was supporting her son and his two grieving children, after their mother died after a brief struggle with cancer. Sharon was struggling with her own loss and told me her seven-year-old granddaughter, Kelly would not talk about her mum. Kelly was refusing the adults' expectations of 'appropriate' emotional expression. Five-year-old Mark, spoke of nothing but Mum, reassuring everyone else that, 'Mum hasn't gone far'.

Sharon brought Mark to one of her sessions to help us finish off a colourful play activity. We had been creating something for the children to help externalise the story of their loss. On a large purple cardboard sheet, we glued bright cut-out houses. We drew roads joining the hospital, relatives' homes and their school (which had a chapel attached where the funeral was held). Mark's job was to put the gold heart stickers on the little cut-out figures and paste the cotton wool clouds at the top. He added some of his own things. We put velcro dots behind the figures and at other places.

When Mark proudly took the scene home, it was dinner time. Sharon told me that Dad put dinner on hold, and they all sat around the coffee table. Kelly became engaged and drew her two cats into the collage. Then she rushed off to get some coloured paper. Kelly cut out a third cat, and put it with mum, up in the clouds, and said, 'Mum will be looking after Tinkerbell now'.

I asked Sharon to speak with the childrens' teachers. Each created a mural of 'Life Changes' in their classroom. Every child could cut out coloured cardboard in the shape of an important person or pet they can't see anymore. The children were encouraged to share fond memories of times spent with precious people and pets. Through this, Kelly found a community of others who she could speak with about her mum.

Sometimes, I tell a story in counselling. Not one I've made up, or one that will 'solve' someone's problems, but a story woven with magic or mystery, and perhaps some wisdom. Each person will take something different from a story. In our final session, I told Sharon the story of Vasilisa. In this Russian fairytale, a dying mother gives her child a little doll. The full story and sketch for learning prompts can be found on my website, including a pattern to make the small dolls.

We then made each child a tiny fabric doll, and I recorded the story for the children. Children need to find stories of hope, where other small people like themselves have overcome grief and rejection, and have found their way to a resolution and a happy ending. I asked Sharon to ask the children, 'What words of comfort to help you through hard times would Mummy have woven into your doll?' These conversations follow Michael White's style of questions found in his article, 'Saying hullo again: The incorporation of the lost relationship in the resolution of grief' where he suggests we aim to stay connected, and find ways to 'say hello' to our loved ones.

If a child wishes, I print out the story, and they can create drawings about the story. They are drawn to parts in the story that begin a healing process for them. Vasilisa's situation is unique, yet every child steps into the central character's shoes, finding strength from Vasilisa's surviving in the face of unfair losses and hurts.

I don't often recommend picture books to clients, as a child can sometimes refuse to hear a so-called 'therapeutic' story from a parent who is struggling with their own distress. However, if we can make contact with the teacher, a story may be read to the whole class.

With Sharon's grandchildren, I recommended, and shared my copy of *The Elephant's Pillow*. Author, Diana Reynolds Roome had been told this story by her own father, and it is illustrated beautifully by Jude Daly. It is about a boy called Li, son of a wealthy merchant who is bored and lonely. One day he hears of an elephant who has not been able to sleep since the death of his master, the old Emperor. The boy urgently sets out on a quest, and his curiosity, compassion, connection and perseverance brings healing to them both.

Developmental changes around grief and loss

- 2–6 years: Children may blow a dandelion clock to 'show mummy where I am'. The fantasy and magical thinking of this stage overlaps with what many call, 'new age' ideas about the spirit's post-death journey. The wish to stay connected feels natural, and can be very helpful.
- 7–10 years: With increasing cognitive awareness, death can suddenly feel like a literal, final and permanent ending to life. This shift to the left brain/analysis/black and white/true or false assessment of the world can be overwhelming. Ambiguity or magical thinking is pushed away. Fears about death can increase.
- 10–14 years: Young people have heard and read more about death. They can develop philosophical questioning about life. 'Why did that happen? Why did he choose to do that?'
- 15–20 years: At this stage, young people often show little interest in bereavement, as they have entered a more self-centred phase. There can be a blind invincibility and sense of immortality which may lead to recklessness and irreverence about the gift of life.

Disenfranchised grief

After a miscarriage, a family death by suicide or public shaming of a parent's private life, a parent may struggle to manage their own, and their child's grief and confusion. Parents whose children have a diagnosis that will delay developmental milestones may experience a loss without an end. They may deeply feel the unfairness of Life, its ability to disrupt their expectations and hopes for their child, and their parenting journey. When a parent succumbs to an often slow, life-changing disease such as cancer, MND or MS, the children can respond to this loss through symptoms such as regression and anger. Many losses and the associated suffering are sometimes not validated or understood by others.

Loss after family violence

Violence around the home can create disenfranchised grief because talking about the problem with friends may be unthinkable as it would bring up feelings of shame. Children need a safe and predictable environment with a protective adult. Children need reassurance that they are loved and the abuse was not their fault. Adults can suggest that talking with a counsellor might be helpful to find safe ways to understand and express their sadness and frustrations.

Depression and risk

Sadness will pass, but sometimes a child can't shake the feeling of sadness. This could mean they are sliding into a depression. This may include feeling numb, helpless and distant from others. There may be unseen self-harm, or thoughts of suicide even in children as young as eight. A timely referral to a GP and psychologist may be the best course of action if the case seems to be beyond the counsellor's area of competence (see Appendix 1).

With adolescents, losses can become more serious in their impact on mental health, especially with peer suicide, relationship breakdowns, loss of safety due to cyberbullying or sexting, loss of integrity due to being involved in a crime, loss of a sporting dream or career hopes, or a realisation that the seriousness of 'adulting' looms as an end to carefree childhood. I make sure every teenager has a 24/7 phone support line in their phone, and I explain what will happen when they call, and explain that one day they may end up using this number for a friend too.

Parents can be coached to begin a risk assessment. They may find this confronting, but you could ask them to practise first or record themselves asking the questions. The simple questions may include, 'Honey you're just not yourself. This has been a year of disappointment and upset. Can I ask you a question? Have you been having thoughts that you don't want to live in this pain? Have you been doing anything to hurt yourself? You know I'm always here for you. I'll check in later, and I hope you'll feel it's okay to talk'. Parents can also call Parentline or Kids Helpline for support.

Cutting

Responding to numbness and loss of control in their life may lead young people to begin cutting. I may introduce a brief history of cutting, including records from the 1800s, of women using their sewing needles to pierce their skin. This assists the young person to reposition themselves, engage their curiosity and remove some of the shame or stigma. 'How does a young person come to choose cutting?'

I ask, 'What other options are available to you?' We can ask a child what other people have suggested, so we know what the child already 'knows' and we will not then add to this burden, or we can become curious and scale the child's response to these. Children may have no idea how they can shift the pattern.

'As you start to walk on the way, the way appears.'
Rumi

Sometimes drawing a diagram which uses the whole brain can facilitate a conversation to broaden the young person's understanding of their personal agency.

I ask the child to draw a crossroads. To the left, the road leads to 'cutting', to the right it leads to 'self-care' (or another word the young person prefers). 'What does care for self look like? Could some hand cream be kept in the place where the scissors are kept, to be a further reminder of your choice to follow the self-care path? What would it mean to you, if you were the one who had the final say about this part of your life, and not let the situation which is troubling you score against you?'

Another increasingly used technology intervention is the Calm Harm award winning app by Stem4 which has four categories: distract, comfort, express and release. It is recommended for children aged 12 years plus.

Case study: It's my fault they separated

Lilly is a nine-year-old 'only' child who realised she'd been keeping herself in a positive mood and holding on to hope that her parents would reunite. Like most children, Lilly felt she was to blame, and her fear was that her parents would stay separated. 'It's my fault they separated because I have been spending too much time on my iPad.' She clung on to the hope that once they saw she would turn off her iPad when asked, and they knew that her happiness depended on them being together again, all would be well.

Lilly drew pizza pictures of why adults might not stay together. She played out her fears and thoughts using puppets and animal genogram play, as well as sand tray expressive activities. Then she drew a future oriented pizza picture with toppings that included 'Mum doesn't like to be with Dad' and 'I will be okay'. Her fears had turned to sadness, 'Now I have lost that hope'.

Since scaling everything helps me stay curious, and I never assume I somehow 'know' how a child feels, I asked Lilly to show me with her outstretched arms how big her hope was at the beginning that her parents would stay together, when she first heard the news. Her arms were wide. Then I asked her to show me how much hope she had now. Lilly's arms came together, but not quite touching. There was a thread of hope still, as is appropriate for a nine-year-old.

This unique moment of self-understanding about Lilly's process through loss was liberating for her, and she was no longer as confused or afraid. Being surrounded by images on the counselling walls of 'two house families' and having therapeutic playtimes to explore her emotions, meant her situation and the sadness were normalised. Lilly did not need additional sessions.

Case study: A deep sleep

Two boys, Mason, 11, and Sean, 12, were struggling with a sudden family separation. In the third session, I told them a story of *Sleepyhead Taro*, as it seemed to parallel what Mum had said about the boys behaving like 'zombie grumpy bums' and seeming stuck.

In the story, Taro lives alone with his mother, in a land stricken with drought. When she suddenly dies, he stops tending the rice paddies on their farm and falls into a deep sleep. He sleeps for three years, and when he wakes to the ongoing drought, he decides to cut a channel for water to flow from a river a long way away to the village, so the people could enjoy good health and happiness.

Sean drew a cartoon of Taro weeping over his mother, then Taro falling into a big, deep sleep before going to dig the channel from the river to water the crops.

Kim: What stood out in the story for you?
Sean: The big sleep was what I thought was interesting.

Cartoon strip (11 years old)

The mother dies. Taro is crying beside her.

Taro sleeps for 3 years. Nobody can wake him.

Taro wakes up and digs a channel from the river to the village so the plants won't die

Tamar Dolev©

Kim: Why do you think that part was significant to you?
Sean: Well, we still have our mum. She loves us and she wants to help us. We are just as sad as Taro.
Mason: We need time to work out why Dad's leaving us.
Kim: So, love is important to you, and maybe you 'Need Time' to work through things? Could you tell me a story about love and when you have maybe helped someone through a hard time?
Sean: Our dog died last year, and Dad was really sad. We helped him dig the hole.
Kim: Why did you decide to help?

Mason: Well Mum was busy with our baby brother, and we all loved our dog. We were all happy back then, and helping dig the hole was hard work, but it got some of the sadness out.
Kim: So, would you say that Loving and Helping and Hard Work are important in your family?
Sean: Yes! And we do help Mum with stuff, 'cos now she has to do everything! We put the bins out ... and wash the car ...
Kim: I'm hearing a story about two boys who have suffered a shock, just like Taro. But it sounds like you're finding ways to live your lives around what is important to you: You're noticing people needing help, and you're giving what you can. Have you got any ideas about how you might deal with some of the problems we talked about last week: Grumpy, Sadness and Shut Down?
Sean: I want to wake up and not be shut down. I'm good with our baby brother, and I've been helping Mum more.
Mason: Well, the story makes me think I'm not as shut down as I was at first: as when we first found out. I am getting awake too. I don't want to be a 'grumpy bum' forever! (The boys laugh, as that's Mum's phrase for their current behaviour.)
Kim: Is 'Working to Help People' something you, and Taro have found can help shift Sadness?

Sean: I'm still really sad Dad left us. And I was pretty angry at what he did. But now if I'm grumpy or sad, at least I know why. It helps looking at the sadness Taro felt, and how he woke up when he was ready to.

'He who has never had a sorrow cannot speak words of comfort.'
Proverb from Uganda

Summary

Grief is shrouded in unspoken rules that dictate expression of emotion. Our job is not to take someone's pain away; rather, we can learn to sit beside them in their grief. We might invite participation in clever interventions, but what most tell me is that just having this safe place to talk is what helped. Then we can ask, 'How has having someone to listen been helpful?'

Actions to take as a result of reading this chapter

1. Make a grief and loss journey map of your own life (see Chapter 8), and especially reflect on what you were going through at the same age as a client you are currently seeing.

2. Spend some time looking at the resources on the following websites which you can then engage in and use as discussion points with young people:

    - Kid's Helpline (https://kidshelpline.com.au/)
    - Seasons of Grief (http://seasonsofgrief.com.au/)
    - Good Grief (https://www.goodgrief.org.au/)
    - Positive Psychology (https://positivepsychology.com/art-therapy/)
    - National Centre for Childhood Grief (https://childhoodgrief.org.au/).

3. For out-of-home care, research Life Story work to document the stories of birth families and foster families (see https://www.berrystreet.org.au/therapeutic-life-story-work for more information).

CHAPTER 8

Therapeutic Stories

'A hero is a man or woman who has been able to battle past his personal and local historical limitations, and return to us, to teach the lesson s/he has learned of life renewed.'

JOSEPH CAMPBELL,
THE HERO WITH A THOUSAND FACES

Therapeutic stories have been scattered like Ananse's ideas (Chapter 4) throughout this book. In this chapter you will find out why. I use stories of heroic journeys because the gravity of a hero's problem often resonates with a child's own situation, and this can open sparkling new conversations.

A story is a walking, talking metaphor that comes alive in the telling. When it is told in the sacred space of therapy, there can be additional magical enchantments. There is ample research which shows heroes can become the blueprint for identity development. Our clients are often confronting serious, and what feels like insurmountable problems. Like the central character of countless stories, they may experience strong feelings of fear, anger, loss and despair.

Storytelling provides a safe emotional work-out: breathing slows down, and the nervous system is calmed as the story concludes. As Babette Rothschild explains in *8 Keys to Safe Trauma Recovery*, establishing control and naming an ending to trauma is helpful in recovery. Indeed, in most stories the hero takes on more control which leads to survival, success and resolution.

Story Medicine has many distinct aspects: the art of selecting and telling the story, the implicit messages woven into the story, the listener's emotional connections to the characters, the 'turning over' of the story in their mind, and sometimes the magical 'ah-ha' of a new understanding of how to address a problem.

Stories from every culture have common archetypes. Also, the hero's quest and how the hero *responds* to the crisis usually follows a similar pattern:

1. A challenge is confronted (the hero feels shock and fear)
2. No success immediately (discouragement)
3. Struggle (hopeful, effort, energetic action taken)
4. Find allies and powers (encouragement)
5. Confront evil (bravery, cleverness)
6. Taste defeat—dark night of the soul (despair)
7. Leap of faith (hope reborn, vision of outcome)

THERAPEUTIC STORIES

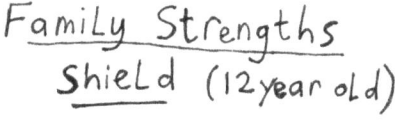

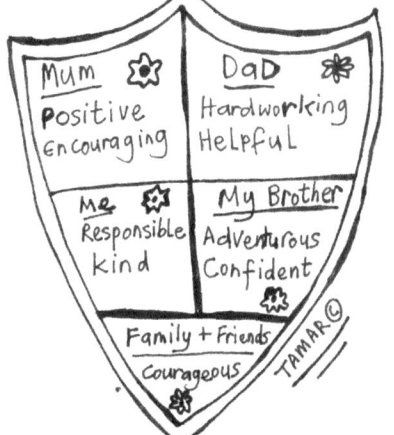

8. Persistent effort (conviction—often the 'third time' brings success)
9. Victory (peace, forgiveness, acceptance and justice).

How might folktales or stories be helpful?

Folktales are helpful because they describe the struggles of an everyday character whose journey includes change and movement forwards, often with helpers along the way. From the beginning, hope is sustained, and a positive resolution is anticipated—two things a therapist knows can support people after trauma.

Listening to a story can stir up a sense of new strength and a shield of identity can be drawn.

Folktales are simpler than complex mythical tales, but they both follow the stages of the 'Hero's Journey' identified by Joseph Campbell. These traditional stories are woven from distilled experiences of many generations and dressed in rich symbols and metaphors. As a child listens, they can face the reality that life is filled with everything: suffering, hopes, failure, wishes and courage, as people navigate towards their need for love, connection and a place in the world.

'if you want to learn to ride a horse—you must also know how to fall.'
Proverb

I often tell therapeutic stories during counselling. I allow children to talk freely afterwards of what they found interesting, offering paper to draw their own images, as I did with Mason and Sean in Chapter 7, or asking a question sometimes the following week. Stories do not deliver a fixed message, rather the listener's mind becomes active and curious, searching for relevance to their own situation.

This work led me to train others in Therapeutic Storytelling. I also have developed a series of questions from the narrative lens to further unpack what the person found in the story and how that might be relevant to them.

Unpack questions after a story

- In what ways did you connect with the identity of the hero of the story?
- In what ways did you relate to the journey of the hero?
- What understandings about your own predicament have you drawn from the story?
- What in the story stands out as important to you?
- In visualising the story, which scenes or characters were you most drawn to?
- How might you now be feeling about hope, or future possibilities after hearing the story?
- What effect has there been on your identified personal issues after listening to the story?
- In what ways might aspects of the hero's experience be validating or helpful for your own heroic journey? (e.g. loss, isolation, jealousy, hopelessness, fear, anger, shame,

despair, inferiority, outcast, unfairness, resentment, new courage, forgiveness, etc.).

Four examples of how a story told can facilitate change

Lionheart: Young people need inspirational stories. Many have sat spellbound and feel reinvigorated and motivated after listening to me retell a short version of how Jesse Martin, a local Melbourne teenager, sailed solo around the world. Jesse's book, *Lionheart* is his story of dreaming of adventure, ignoring the naysayers, meeting challenges, applying effort, stumbling, holding on to hopes and overcoming self-doubt. He endured moments of terror and powerlessness, months of isolation, depression and despair until he achieved his purpose and returned after his single-handed sail around the world. Children need stories where the seemingly impossible becomes possible.

> *'Everything is possible until proven impossible,*
> *and then you just need to become more creative.'*
> **Scott Parazynski, *The Sky Below***

Arnie: Another real-life story I share is Arnold Schwarzenegger's. Arnie set out from Austria as a young man to cross the threshold into his dreams. He became a champion bodybuilder, famous movie star and more recently, Governor of California. In 2018 he gave a motivational speech in Germany, where he asks his audience: 'What direction are you heading? What is your purpose? What is your goal? Only 25 per cent enjoy the work they are doing! What is your vision? Don't listen to the naysayers!'

Bear Grylls: This is a very brief anecdote I sometimes share that gets a young person reflecting about their fears, and how they might respond to them:

Bear Grylls is a celebrity and former SAS serviceman and survival instructor. He says, 'I'm scared of heights and cocktail parties'. He has to renew his decision to confront challenges every day.

Geraldine

Geraldine asked for a new story each week, to ease her mental and physical pain as she was having cancer treatment. One day I told her the story of *The Servant at the Palace* (from Chapter 3) which concludes with healing water being released. In the story there are many themes I thought might resonate with her life: isolation, rejection, powerlessness, daunting hierarchies, following one's interest and holding on to hope.

A week after telling this story, Geraldine became distressed waiting for a painful procedure at the hospital, where the chemotherapy bag and a 'thick' needle port would be stitched into her shoulder. She said, 'I knew I had to do something else to help myself'. She found herself visualising, and drawing on a metaphor from the story where the healing water was revealed. 'I suddenly saw that the chemotherapy fluid was my very own "healing water of life", and this changed how I felt. I stopped being afraid and felt grateful I could have this. I watched every step of the procedure with curiosity. After that, I didn't experience any pain.'

> Geraldine was a courageous hero on her journey with cancer. She then became a helper, sharing with others at the oncology clinic the story of The Servant.

'A hero is an ordinary individual who finds the strength to persevere and endure in spite of overwhelming obstacles.'
Christopher Reeve

How to use therapeutic storytelling

Of course, the client comes to us to tell their own story—and a narrative therapist will ask questions which help them think differently about their experiences, and articulate their values and hopes. This can help them to view their story from a new angle, and allow them to tell it in a way that makes them stronger.

This approach is not a trick or reframe. Narrative therapy uses the externalising strategy as the starting point, creating space for the person to reposition themselves in relation to their problem.

In the overlap between a person's life journey and the hero's journey from a story told, the vitality in the hero to keep persevering and moving forward, crosses over into the person's desire to shift or get through a troubling problem. They can find nourishment from a folktale or anecdote, along with the images and meanings they have independently created from listening to the story, and so discover an inspirational, fresh possibility.

In Chapter 6, I shared a case where I used what is called the 'mutual storytelling technique' with nine-year-old Daniel. This gives a child a sense of control, which is another well-known trauma recovery tool.

As I was developing my interest in using folktales, I took Joseph Campbell's Hero Journey framework, and adapted it for therapy. It provides a scaffolding and captures new perspectives of a person's strengths, learnings and the purposes of their own journey.

I also wrote an article for *Counselling Australia Journal* which introduces 'Therapy as a Journey' using these principles (https://www.theaca.net.au/journals/ACAMagVol21No2.pdf).

As the client listens to a heroic journey, there is often some sparkling image from the story told by the counsellor that awakens a fresh way of looking at the person's life. They can use the Hero Map to further unpack their own stages, helpers, and possible ways ahead. I have developed a colourful, child's version of Joseph Campbell's Hero's Journey, illustrated by Simon Hudson which is available as a PDF on my website, and there are many others available on the internet.

THERAPEUTIC STORIES

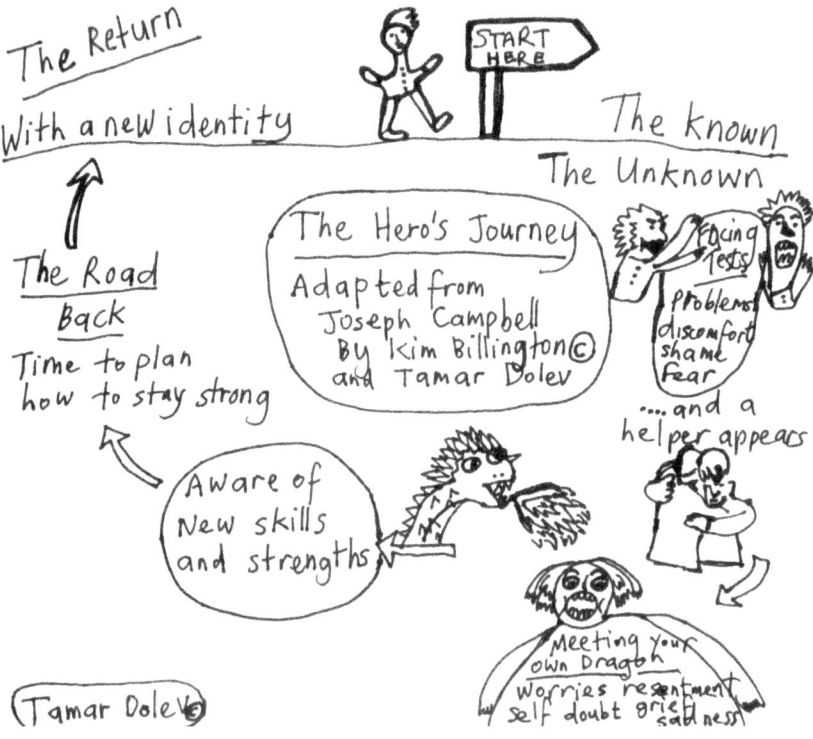

As the hero develops through their journey, post-traumatic growth is revealed. The hero encounters obstacles, suffers, is afraid and awakens to recognise right from wrong. The hero is willing to take actions to move forwards with courage, determination and purpose towards a fair and just resolution.

> *'Stories are the pathway to engaging our right brain and triggering our imagination. By engaging our imagination, we become participants in the narrative. We can step out of our own shoes, see differently, and increase our empathy for others. Through imagination, we tap into creativity that is the foundation of innovation, self-discovery and change.'*
> **Pamela Rutledge**

At the beginning of any story, the hero isn't a hero yet

Luke Skywalker wanders the sand dunes of his aunt and uncle's farm in Tatooine; Frodo and friends are living easy in the Shire; Harry Potter is locked under the stairs. They each are in the 'known' land, similar to the year 2019, before the coronavirus pandemic.

Then, something bursts into the characters' lives to call them out of their ordinary, everyday existence into a journey that changes everything. Journeys may involve leaving home, stretching boundaries, trusting unknown helpers, and mastering new tools for difficulties ahead.

Joseph Campbell studied myths and their relevance to man. He discovered that the motifs and patterns of the heroic journey were universal, and even found in our everyday lives. We leave the safety of the ordinary world and enter the belly of the whale, the dark times where the certainties we expect to have around us ... are missing!

Stories of heroic struggles hold hidden powers to energise and inspire discovery about what is possible as a human, and how one might make sense of life's tribulations. The hero is the model for vitality, perseverance, growth and change.

> *'The world breaks everyone, and afterward, many are strong in the broken places.'*
> **Ernest Hemmingway**

Children and young people who have experienced a trauma or loss can be overwhelmed by worries and uncertainty. They enter a time 'in limbo,' which is found in every traditional story too. There are three stages identified using the lens of the 'rites of passage' metaphor:

1. separation from the known, (associated with a loss of identity)
2. a limbo, liminal, 'betwixt and between' period of confusion and discomfort
3. the arrival at a new status with new responsibilities.

Life moves children from one state to another, such as transition to high school, sexual maturation stages, year 12 to freedom. The middle space offers a fresh possibility for a person to reinterpret and reposition themselves in their lives, and to choose a new direction or attitude for their new 'alternative' future story. There are always 'helpers' along the way.

Helpers

Heroes in traditional tales are often helped along their way by imaginative characters such as the wind, or a talking animal, and children are fine with this, just as we as adults suspend belief when reading a novel or watching a computer-generated film.

Who are the people or pets who help your client? What difference have they made? We can ask them who is their hero, and then ask, 'Who is your hero's helper?' It could be that your client identifies as both a hero and a helper on their journey. From our periods in isolation during the COVID-19 lockdown, we learned we need others. The reassurance of a friendly voice or face on Zoom helped fulfil our basic human need for connection.

'It is important to reflect upon the fact that the need for co-regulation never goes away in any of our lives. Think about the last time you had a crisis in your life and were helped by another calmer human brain that provided you with a soothing presence and you felt a sense of safety because of your relationship with this person.'
Lori Desautels & Michael McKnight

There are many cyclic metaphors that I've used to bring to a child the images of change and growth: from the cycle of the seasons, to a seed growing into a fruit tree, or a drop of water emerging from a spring in a mountainside, that cascades down waterfalls until it arrives at a river and flows into the sea. Each loses itself as change happens and the surprising transformations bring vitality to the person's imagination.

How does a caterpillar turn into a butterfly?

A caterpillar must first digest itself! But certain groups of cells survive, turning the caterpillar soup into eyes, wings, antennae and other structures that become the butterfly.

The famous Eric Carle story begins with a very hungry caterpillar hatching from an egg. The caterpillar feeds on leaves, growing plumper and shedding its skin. One day, the caterpillar stops eating, hangs upside down from a twig and spins itself a silky cocoon. Inside this protective casing, even more magic happens as the caterpillar transforms its body, and emerges as a butterfly. Telling this story can be therapeutic.

A child might not know they are on a heroic journey

Children and young people can sometimes be scrambling to gather power and influence after years of oppression. I recall a supervisee talking about a 16-year-old who was deemed 'rebellious'. He had entered into a drug gang, but he was still attending school. I wondered if the boy might find the drawing of The Crossroads helpful, to reflect and name the different pathways he could choose. I suggested he be asked, 'How confident are you about the choice you've made to be with this gang? Is it in line with your values?'

The boy later declared he was not actually happy on his current course. He shared his dream. He wanted to live a good life, take up a trade, and build his own house so that when he was 30, he could have a family and support them. The crossroads journey metaphor opened up a visible new direction which encapsulated his hidden hopes and wishes.

Indigenous cultures and story therapy

I have been integrating the work of Lewis Mehl-Madrona, MD into my work. He points out that within most indigenous cultures, the mind is not considered separately from body, community and spirituality, unlike the silos created in the dominant western culture. Healing must involve the mind, body, the community, and the spirits. His goal is to bring the wisdom of indigenous peoples about healing back into mainstream medicine and to transform medicine and psychology through this wisdom coupled with more European derived narrative traditions.

His work shows that neuroscience is catching up with indigenous people's understandings, and that the default mode of the brain is telling stories. He quotes a neuroscientist at the University of Montreal, who explains how the story of Little Red Riding Hood contains tremendously more information than a 20-digit number, and asks us, 'Which is easier to remember?'

As Mehl-Madrona says, 'The stories we tell ourselves are changing our physiology every time we tell them. If you can see that in real time, you can begin to draft better stories'. This aligns with the narrative therapy techniques of discovering alternative stories of strengths and values, and using them in re-authoring conversations.

Troubling thoughts

I often find myself saying, 'Are Troubling Thoughts living "rent-free" in your head?' After a smile, we might perform a rental inspection, and see what trouble they're up to. I like to use this short story to begin a conversation about how these uninvited thoughts came to be. I suggest children imagine swooping a net and catching a thought, and then ask: 'What is that thought doing for you? Is it taking you on the right path? If not, then how might you show it the door!' One boy said, 'I'll blow the whistle, give it a red card and send it off!'

Two Wolves is a well-known Cherokee (First Nation American Indian) legend which illustrates the battle between our helpful and hurtful thoughts. I write the emotion words on cards and invite reflection about which might be dominant in a child's life.

> *An old Cherokee is teaching his grandchild about life.*
> *'A fight is going on inside me,' he said. 'It's a terrible fight and it is between two wolves. One is evil—he is anger, envy, sorrow, regret, greed, arrogance, self-pity, guilt, resentment, inferiority, lies, false pride, superiority and ego.'*

He continued, 'The other is good—he is joy, peace, love, hope, serenity, humility, kindness, benevolence, empathy, generosity, truth, compassion and faith. The same fight is going on inside you—and inside every other person, too'.

The grandchild thought about it for a minute and then asked the grandfather, 'Which wolf will win?'

The old Cherokee simply replied, 'The one you feed'.

Stories can sensitively and matter-of-factly present the dark and light opposites of life's experiences, opening up conversations about how we might be inwardly striving for growth.

Summary

Storytelling in therapy can engage the child's interest, sidestep resistance, enable them to safely reconnect with, express and make sense of their feelings on their journey. Focus can be shifted from current problem-saturated self-talk and concerns, to keeping hope alive, widening the perspective on problems and creating new strategies.

Folktales recruit our imagination, and by expanding our own horizons, they help capture unexpected solution possibilities for our own story.

Stories of heroic struggles hold hidden powers to energise and inspire discovery about what is possible. They show how one might make sense of life's tribulations. The hero is the model for vitality, perseverance, growth and change. Myths, folktales and fairytales are woven with symbolic metaphors and archetypal characters. They make a potent medicine for inspiring hope and courage on life's journey.

Actions to take as a result of reading this chapter

1. Select any story that has caught your own interest in the book, and ask yourself, 'Why did that journey or those images capture my attention?' Write down the bones of the story, sketch each stage and without learning it by rote, walk around reading the images in your head.

2. Take the plunge, and ask a client this week, 'Would you be interested in hearing a small story that might be relevant to something you've been experiencing?' Tell the story then use the unpack questions found earlier in the chapter on page 142.

3. If you feel you're not up to telling a story to begin with, you may be interested in another oral tradition, such as writing a few proverbs on pieces of paper, and creating a Lucky Dip Jar of Wisdom.

CHAPTER 9

Power Rules

'No-one is you and that is your power.'

DAVE GROHL

This chapter may possibly make the biggest difference in your practice. When children, or adults experience life problems, they may feel embarrassed or ashamed. They may default to a conclusion they are a 'failure' or they are not 'normal.' Other people may criticise, and focus on and reinforce this one aspect of their lives. After a while, this dominant problem story is used to describe them. Someone else is getting to write their story. Someone else is making conclusions about their lives. Does this seem like a balanced, fair power dynamic?

Many referrals come with a behaviour tag which suggests the child has not kept themselves in their alotted place in the pecking order, or has not worked hard enough to fit in to the parent's expectations.

From the moment a child is born they are subject to the power of the adults and older siblings around them. Parents get to choose a child's name, and there can be competing power influences as grandparents vie for the middle names. Each child's story is evidence of how they have been shaped socially and globally.

It took me a few years to address this power issue fully in the counselling room, and in my consultations with parents. A family cannot be a 'democracy' as children first need to be coached, gradually, to understand that rights come with responsibilities. However, year by year, their voice and wishes can increasingly be considered by those with the vested power of parenthood. Parents cannot hold on to power until a child is 18, but they often do not think through how they will incrementally reach that end point.

Externalising the problem is one thing, but without an assessment of the family dynamics, we shall not get very far. Child-blaming descriptions that would be shame-inducing, may end up being bigger than the original problem. We have all been children, and can recall how there were many times in our lives when we were afraid or hurt by others. Can you recall a name that was the label you were known by?

We can explore how every minute is filled with a thousand choices about how to think, feel and act. We can assist children by validating their strengths, values and actions, without always offering our praise for their achievements, but rather ask them how they feel about their achievements. 'So, tell me how that team success/school grade/tidy room is feeling for you?'

*'I am not what happened to me,
I am what I choose to become.'*
Carl Jung

Responding to Harm

Many children experience being physically and verbally abused and see acts of violence. Sometimes, someone notices something. Perhaps there is some cutting? (see Chapter 7). As counsellors, where do we begin? Of course we must prioritise and assess for risk, and ensure we are clear about mandatory reporting of abuse and neglect, and the need to recognise cumulative harm, or imminent risk (see Appendix 1). But, we can do so much more.

Any behaviour is communication. Cutting, for example represents something. The young person has made a step in a new direction. It may mean they have made a decision to take back control. We can help them understand their fears and the rage at any unjust treatment they have endured, and we can assist them with understanding some of the power dynamics they are subject to. These discussions lead to a sense of validation and confidence we can be with them through this tumultuous time as they transition to adulthood.

'Power is always temporary.'
Martin Firrell

Case study: I've had enough

Alice is a 15-year-old girl who has been sent to counselling by a teacher who has seen scratches on her arm. Staff know there have been problems at home for years, but Alice is a model student, so they now are very worried. In her second appointment, Alice says, 'I use a fruit knife because it's not sharp. When I cut, I think to myself, "I want it to end"'.

I ask more about the meaning of the fruit knife, and why she selected that one, not the butter knife or another one. Alice has something to say, and is building up the courage to say it using whatever means she can. In her second appointment, Alice says, 'This cut says, "I've had enough of being hit and yelled at. That's enough!"' Alice writes 'That's Enough!' on a sticky note and pins it to the pin up board, amongst other cryptic code words accumulated over time by young people.

I suggest to Alice that she is looking uplifted by her act of rebellion. 'I can't change him (her father), but I can change me.' I ask what these changes might look like. Alice shares she wants to study law and help women in these kinds of marriages. This new generation are becoming aware that women no longer have to stay in an abusive relationship, where men feel entitled to hold power and dominance.

The following week the father was interviewed by Child Protection, and booked himself in to attend a Men's Anger Management class. Some weeks later, Alice drew a Tree of Life (see Chapter 11).

Alice decided to adopt a sticky note prompt from the wall: *Will this add value?* When I asked a scaling question of 'How much value will it add having that note from another student? Alice said it meant twice as much as what an adult could offer. Alice later reported this tiny paper note reduced the urge to cut, as she felt she was not alone.

Alice's final work was drawing an image about taking back her power, and not letting people live rent-free in her head. The metaphor of choosing your tenants was light-hearted, and she was happy to keep such forward thinking hopes alive with her colourful drawing.

Power and identity are never fixed. There are always some shifts possible, hence the relentless, magical externalising, 'why,' 'how' and scaling questions we ask with the intention to ascertain a person's strengths, skills, values, beliefs and hopes for the future.

Computer games invite players to develop skills to achieve power

Parents wonder why children love computer games. One reason is that their game skills are rewarded regardless of a previous error last week. They are granted more power as they score highly, in accordance to the rules of engagement. Children can accept the consequences of their poor decisions, or ineffective attempts to achieve their goal, when consequences are not personally dished out, but given to all players. Everything is immediate and clear. There is disappointment, but they get to choose what game they play tomorrow.

This is not so in family dynamics. Power is often wielded unfairly, slyly or unconsciously. The structures of power are often not transparent. Young people can be shamed and reminded of their misbehaviours months after an incident, so they can't shake off a failure. This style of parenting could be a trans-generational pattern.

Adolescents push back

We find in counselling that when children reach adolescence, they already have so much to push back against. Examples of rage, or surrender and depression have been seen in the case studies presented in previous chapters. When children are subject to injustices, abuse and undue constraint, they begin to rebel. They may express this outwardly, or inwardly towards themselves.

A vivid example of power tussles is a scene towards the end of the film, *Mary Poppins* (https://youtube/E6ADGIHIKnI). Mr Banks is looking for someone to blame, as his career is in crisis. He arrives home to a tsunami of chimney sweeps shaking his hand. He digs in his heels, and chooses his battle to re-establish his power and control in the home. (He has previously crowed, 'It's grand to be an Englishman in 1910: King Edward's on the throne, it's the Age of Men, I'm the lord of my castle, the sovereign, the liege'.) Now, he turns to Mary Poppins:

> Mr Banks: (sternly) Just a moment, Mary Poppins! What is the meaning of this outrage?
> Mary Poppins: I beg your pardon?
> Mr Banks: Will you be good enough to explain all this?
> Mary Poppins: First of all, I would like to make one thing perfectly clear.
> Mr Banks: Yes?
> Mary Poppins: I never explain anything.

Here we see an example of how men have been brought up with the desire for, or sense of entitlement for, power and influence in a home, school or work setting. Children know what this is, but we can pause in our counselling space and name it. Children may say, 'I wish I had courage like Mary Poppins, to stand up to Mr Banks'. But there's so much more in this vignette.

Fear Response

In session, we may watch the 34-second clip together (on screen or in person). In a family session we can unpack each person's fear responses to bids by others to dominate. Children soon see that the adults around them may be using anger, blame and intimidation to control them. (Family sessions can only proceed when a family violence risk assessment has been made.)

When children feel trapped, or their right to safety is dismissed, children's brains may choose one of three paths:

POWER RULES

1. Fight: They find a way to create havoc until they are heard

2. Flight: An active, non-violent resistance (e.g. a child refuses to attend school where bullying is happening)

3. Freeze: They curl up in a shell and can slide into a depression.

I often say, 'A family cannot be a "democracy" with equal final-say decisions, since parents bear this burden of responsibility for what happens up to the age of 18. But, sometimes small things can make a big difference. Is everyone up for a discussion about more negotiations around power and responsibility around the home?'

I've used this dialogue as a starting point for when a young person has survived family violence, and they are now in a safe place, but are still struggling. 'Is it true that everyone must comply when one person makes demands? What are ways you would like to contribute to a different way of living together?' These are the enthralling conversations we can include as an everyday part of counselling. We may look at other societal structures, and reflect on how they came to be, such as police powers, or the power of the school principal. These ideas are central to narrative therapy conversations.

Power and control is found in sexting and WhatsApp group chats. Young people have huge 21st century challenges. When supporting a young person (and they can be as young as eight) responding to cyberbullying and online grooming, I also refer to Mary Poppins' assertiveness skills. 'You never have to explain yourself. If you've said, "no" and someone whines, "but, why?" you do not have to answer that. You do not need to accept their invitation, to be drawn back into their web. Instead, you can say, "I said, no".'

The Netflix documentary, *The Social Dilemma* also brings to our awareness how power and control is behind the big social media companies, manipulating 'users' by using algorithms that encourage addiction to their platforms. Personal data is harvested to target users with advertisements. Children have not enough life experiences to grasp the depth of such deviant, evil predators. Parents often seek support when their child has been caught up in the web, and we need to keep up with where children may be at risk.

Creative ways to introduce the concept of power

In my experience, children don't grasp this very basic knowledge about power clearly unless it's pointed out. A bit like a fish does not know what 'water' is. Using the 'circles of influence' to talk through what lies in the person's own realm of control might be helpful.

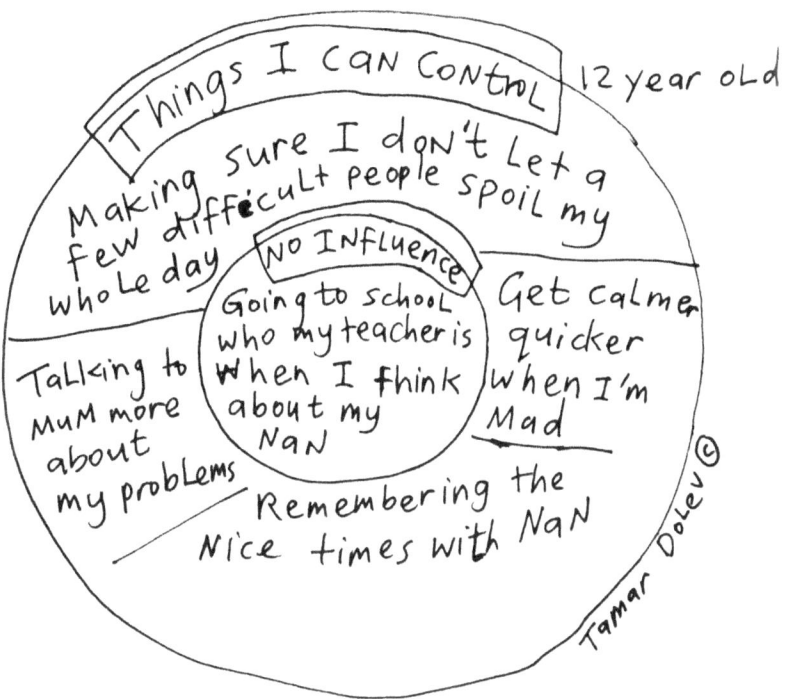

I've also successfully implemented many of the 'Rock and Water' program's strategies, and a three-minute introduction is available at: (https://youtu.be/9CzF98K5OTY).

Lao Tzu offers some ancient wisdom about power and strength:

> 'Water is the softest thing, yet it can penetrate mountains and earth. This shows clearly the principle of softness overcoming hardness.'

The Queen, the Crown and the Storyteller is a lovely short story about living amid challenging, power imbalances, which can be found in Chapter 12.

Using sand tray figurines

With older children I may ask, 'How do people challenge one another in your family? How are things negotiated? What are the power dynamics at home? Let's see if these figurines can show us the problems. Each one can be an important person in your life. Don't forget to include your dog!'

I might also suggest we create 'last year, this year and next year' scenes with the characters, then photograph them and look at them side-by-side. I ask, 'Are you interested in setting up a photo for how something gets tricky at home? We can photo every scene as it unfolds and make an animation film.' (Refer to https://carolinetran.net/how-to-create-easy-stop-motion-animation-photography-with-kids/.)

Bullying

Big problems in children's lives are often created from top-down. Leading world figures and people who gratify their own wishes by abusing others or grooming children, for too long have shown by bad example how to *not* be a decent human. Have you ever watched question time in parliament?

> 'There comes a point where we need to stop just pulling people out of the river. We need to go upstream and find out why they're falling in.'
> **Desmond Tutu**

We know that bullies will only do what bystanders allow, whether this is online, in the workplace or in the family home. The adult role is to guide and support children to become 'upstanders'. We can help them begin to understand power dynamics.

I help children see what happens objectively, in the moment of a bullying incident. How power happens and how it operates strategically. I use puppet play and role rehearsals to help a child understand and consider different responses to the school bully. Especially the bystander's role and the bully's fear of losing status.

In the real world, the child probably does not feel safe enough to act in person, however in counselling, they have shown to themselves that they would if they could. But often it's just not possible.

I ask about a child's favourite movies. I ask why some film characters are drawn to, and then excel in bullying behaviours. We might even write a report card for Darth Vader or another antagonist: 10/10 in intimidation 0/10 in kindness. I introduce the gendered imbalance of power by talking about how in advertising, it is often the male that is buying new cars, so they put a pretty lady next to the car, or in the car. This is what we mean by the objectification of women.

'Nothing discloses real character like the use of power. It is easy for the weak to be gentle. Most people can bear adversity. But if you wish to know what a man really is, give him power. This is the supreme test. It is the glory of Lincoln that, having almost absolute power, he never abused it, except on the side of mercy.'
Robert G. Ingersoll

First nations awareness

I encourage schools to introduce the film, *In My Blood It Runs*. It helps children believe that changes can happen when they are supported by adults. Twelve-year-old Dujuan Hoosan, the central storyteller in the film went to the United Nations Human Rights Council in Geneva, and said: 'I came here to speak to you because the Australian government is not listening, it never listens to kids like me, but we have important things to say ... I want my school to be run by Aboriginal people. I want adults to stop putting 10-year-old kids in jail.'

I also would like to encourage counsellors who are reading this book to stay abreast of all First Nations' troubles. They have suffered gross, historical abuses by people who stole and will not return something precious: their land, their languages and culture, and this disadvantage and dispossession is connected to shockingly high rates of family breakdown, suicide, incarceration and addictions. Things that were unknown until the white boat people arrived 250 years ago.

White domination is an ongoing problem and the refusal to take responsibility by the invaders is being repeated, creating further hardships. I invite the reader to ask themselves, 'Who set the original rules for societal interactions? Who decided what is right and what is wrong? If stealing is wrong, why does England not return the land to indigenous people? Or at least the thousands of artefacts they took and still keep locked up in their museums?' If a neighbour stole your lawn mower, you would want it back.

Although the next story may become an old story soon, it was current at the time of writing and I like to bring current affairs into every session.

Quaden's Story

Nine-year-old Quaden Bayles was relentlessly bullied at school for being different and was vulnerable to targeted meanness and humiliation. An indigenous boy living with a form of dwarfism, he threatened self-harm as a result of his treatment by other children.

In her desperation, Quaden's mother, Yarraka, videoed his distress and shared it on Facebook. The post was seen by thousands of people and it broke their hearts. This led to an offer for Quaden to lead the NRL Indigenous All Stars side onto the ground for their clash with their Maori counterparts on the Gold Coast. The compassion displayed by people in positions of power created opportunities for change in people's awareness and actions to remediate and better the lot for other children.

His extreme duress opened up an opportunity for Quaden's voice to be heard. In a pre-recorded video played at the Royal Commission into Disability, Quaden was asked what message he would give to children who did not understand his disability. He replied: 'Just don't be rude to kids who have disabilities and just be kind and be nice.'

Ms Bayles said Quaden now received more support at school and the bullying had stopped. 'I honestly feel like it took a viral video for us to be able to get the support we need,' she said.

Children in our care also need to know that adults can advocate for them. It is possible to be part of changes, and we can broaden the conversations about ways to take back power.

> *'Our deepest fear is not that we are inadequate.*
> *Our deepest fear is that we are powerful beyond measure.'*
> **Marianne Williamson**

Adolescent abuse towards parents

For many years this has become a growing problem. If a young person seems ready to own their actions which have caused fear and distress to others in the family, I may ask, 'What led to you choosing that course of action over another?' or 'Would you be open to receiving help to becoming accountable for your actions?' or 'Have you begun thinking it's time to make changes?'

These conversations involve discovering what a person's ethics and values are, and what they believe is the fair and right way to treat others, and be treated. These ideas are drawn from the work of Alan Jenkins, and his book *Becoming Ethical* which was a core text during my work as a co-facilitator in Men's Behaviour Change Programs with Relationships Australia and as a telephone counsellor with MensLine.

These approaches have been very helpful in my work where mothers, in particular, are being targeted. Young people may be demanding money for drugs, threatening with knives, physically assaulting or breaking furniture, and so on. Mothers in these situations cannot bear to get the police involved due to shame and fear of escalation.

We can support adolescents to ask themselves, 'What kind of person do I want to become?' Discussions of value include those centred on a person's sense of entitlement in relation to age, gender, race, occupation, etc.

Jenkins uses narrative practices and was influenced by post-structural philosophers such as Deleuze and Foucault. He suggests the direction of healing and restoration needs to be towards men choosing fairness, respect, compassion and accountability. He says it is not possible to embark upon a restorative journey without facing shame. If a person identifies their actions as wrong, that is the acknowledgment of guilt, in a legal context. If they are courageous enough, they can be therapeutically supported to go even further, and face the painful emotion of shame about their harmful attitudes and abuse of power.

Our work with young people who have begun to act in harmful ways may have arrived as a result of a parent taking out a court intervention order against them, or child protection becoming involved. Young people often defend their position, and declare that they themselves were victims to abuse growing up. We can acknowledge that patriarchal structures seem to be giving men licence to hold firmly to male privileges, but I ask, 'You may have a daughter one day. How would you like her to be treated by men?'

My focus with young people who have used violence and abuse, is to avoid collusion and hold on to compassion. 'Early in your life, you experienced unfair and unjust behaviours from others. We might not be able to hold that other person to account. They may show no remorse. So that chapter of unfairness is done. What have you learned from those shocking experiences?'

I may say, 'I feel a deep sadness and shock for the hurt you've caused your mother/sibling. And I'm still with you here, and wanting to support you to find a way to reconstruct your identity, according to what you have learnt is important'.

There are three agreements Jenkins identifies as central to restorative projects when a person uses power and abuse to control others around them. Listed below, they can guide the person to create an appropriate plan of intention.

1. Cessation of violence and abuse

2. Restitution for harm done to the person abused

3. Requests for reclaiming a sense of integrity for the person who has abused

'If you don't believe, to the bottom of your soul, that people are not their problems and that their difficulties are social and personal constructions, then you won't be seeing these transformations. When Epston or White are in action, you can tell they are absolutely convinced that people are not their problems. Their voices, their postures, their whole beings radiate possibility and hope. They are definitely under the influence of optimism.'
Bill O' Hanlon

Summary

In our work, we must uncover the history of The Problem, research the power imbalances locally and globally, and find the preferred ways of living according to the person's values.

We are with our clients for a small fraction of their lives, but our compassion and expertise can support children and their families to throw pebbles into the pond of humanity. We need to believe that these metaphoric ripples can lead to new possibilities of change.

Actions to take as a result of reading this chapter

1. Get informed: research resources based on your locality, for example, 'Youth Law Australia' for providing free, confidential legal information and help for young people under 25 on topics such as sexting and cyberbullying.

2. Find out all you can about school bullying responses by teachers and counsellors.

3. Research the United Nations Convention on the Rights of the Child (https://www.unicef.org.au/Upload/UNICEF/Media/Our%20work/childfriendlycrc.pdf).

CHAPTER 10

Philosophy – Making Sense of Life's Problems

'The best way to make children good is to make them happy.'

OSCAR WILDE

For children, making meaning from chaos and confusion is one of the many developmental tasks of growing up. We listen and watch, we see how others are treated, we reflect on what people say to us, and how they say it. We are constructing knowledges about the ways of the world. This can then allow us to choose our own paths in freedom.

As a counsellor, what is your own understanding of the nature of the world and humans? I have spent decades reflecting on this topic, and my sense is that we are each doing our best with where we are right now on our journey. We sometimes perform actions we may regret. We may have experienced others treating us in hurtful ways. How should we respond to Life?

How else can we learn unless the cosmos gives us the freedom to err. If we want to be offered forgiveness and compassion, then we need to be ready to offer that to others. How do we believe we should live our lives? Most people are unaware of how much freedom we actually have. It's time for an old Buddhist parable:

Choosing to receive a gift

The Buddha was once walking through a village. A young man came up and began saying all kinds of rude words.

However, the Buddha was not upset. He said, 'May I ask you a question? If you have bought a gift for someone, and that person doesn't take it, doesn't want it, who does the gift belong to?'

The young man was surprised to be asked such a strange question and answered, 'It would belong to me, because I bought the gift'.

The Buddha smiled and said, 'That is correct. And this is the same with your anger. I can choose to accept this gift, or decline it. If I do not want to receive it, it will be yours, and yours alone.'

This next story is an old Sufi parable, and brings forth the person's values and hopes and sense of fairness in Life:

The Bag of Walnuts
A Nasruddin story from Persia

Once upon a time there were three children who spent many hours up in a walnut tree. They now had a great sack of walnuts and they took it to the wisest man in their village, Nasruddin, to ask him to divide the nuts among them, as he understood the ways of the world and they had not yet learnt to count.

The sage said, 'Oh you would not like me to do that!' but they pleaded. So he gave the first child one walnut. To the second he gave five walnuts.

Then he gave the rest to the third.

The first two protested, 'That's not fair!'.

Nasruddin said, 'You didn't ask me to be fair. You asked me to distribute them knowing the ways of the world'.

I have a small hessian sack with walnuts in it. I tell this story when I come across children and young people whose lives have not been 'fair' and I have to tell them I have no magic wand. One eight-year-old girl said, 'Kim, you haven't finished the story yet. In the next chapter, the boy with the big pile of walnuts looks at the other piles and says, "This isn't right. Let's make the piles more even".'

This girl was showing me what she believes in and demonstrates that we make decisions based on our beliefs.

Choose any subject: death, suicide, obesity or equality ... and ask yourself, 'How did I develop my belief about this topic?'

Philosophy is the process and result of asking very basic questions about the nature of humans, their thinking, feelings and actions. It includes reflections about the nature of the universe, and how everything connects.

As a counsellor, it is my belief that I am here to be available as a skilled, compassionate resource. Children may be little, but they're already forming their world views. We can ask with curiosity, what the child's ideas are. 'Let's look at this together. How did you choose to manage the problem in that way?'

Each lived experience furthers their wisdom. 'Knowing something about anxiety, what is your theory about helpful ways to support a friend who is struggling with anxiety?' We need to show children we trust them to think for themselves about many things.

Viktor Frankl, who survived the death camps of WWII, said if you can find your own 'why' to life, you will find a 'how' to get through tough times.

Working with parents

> *'Establishing and maintaining partnerships with parents, on behalf of the child, is probably the most complicated, challenging aspect of working with children. At the same time, it is more widely acknowledged than in the past that it is the most important aspect, if one wants to make a lasting impact for the good of the child.'*
> **Prof Anne Stonehouse**

At intake, my assessment is of the family's capacity to come together with intention and willingness for the whole family to grow. When a group can collaborate and name their preferred future, possible next steps forwards emerge, opening doors for meaningful change. Otherwise, parents may revert to an authoritarian parenting style from the last century, top-down dictating of what the family rules are, full stop.

My hope is to find ways to encourage parents to be open to new ideas and adapt their style to each child. I've heard it said that a mind is like a parachute—it works best when it is open.

Questions we can ask a parent are, 'What percentage of perfection are you hoping for in your child?' I may remind them that in every beautiful handmade Persian rug you will find a deliberate mistake.

For surely, only Allah makes things perfectly, and therefore to weave a perfect rug or carpet would be an offence to Allah.

Wabi Sabi is a Japanese word reminding us to look for the beauty and appreciation of things imperfect and impermanent, and accepting the flow of life. I have an image of a broken Japanese bowl in my virtual art gallery power point. The cracks where it broke are now filled with gold.

In family sessions everyone can listen to one another and reflect on their beliefs and hopes, and how they want to live their lives. Online, each person can be sitting in their own space, with their own screen, but still connected.

Recognition of a child's journey

Children facing serious problems get to do advanced classes in Life. They have these lessons in life tucked under their belt, that nobody else can see. They are Ninjas! Children from stable families, with little history of trauma, mental health struggles or financial problems, do not have the opportunity to acquire the black belt of surviving and thriving that we're talking about.

The Yin Yang symbol is a visual reminder about how life works. It is similar to William Blake's poem:

> *'Joy and woe are woven fine, a clothing for the soul divine.'*

At the closure of our counselling work I often recognise such achievements with certificates. These are not difficult to write, because they arise from the unpacking of what the child or young person has shared: what they've been learning, what's important to them, and why. Other times, children spontaneously create something for other children.

When children make artwork in session, if they wish they can leave a copy for the counselling room walls, aka The Art Gallery to share with other clients. They're invited to contribute to a 'Wisdom Book,' and create poems.

In 2017, Zoë, a vibrant 12-year-old came to one of her sessions wearing a yin yang necklace. We researched the ancient symbol in session, and Zoë then spontaneously wrote this amazing poem, adding her understanding to this wisdom. She was excited to share it with others. We made multiple copies and she pinned them to the notice board. Over the years, her poem has been the foundation of changes in many of my adult and child client's lives. I am grateful she and her family agreed to have it included in this book, where it can now reach even more people.

Sometimes you're angry but there's always some happiness.
Sometimes you're happy but there's always some sadness.
Sometimes you're scared but there's always some courage.
Even in the dark night there is always some bright light.
By Zöe 12yrs

Tamar ©

David Epston has a great tradition of people sharing their wisdom on the website Narrative Approaches (http://www.narrativeapproaches.com/resources/anorexia-bulimia-archives-of-resistance/). This is a lifesaving archive of personal stories, essays, poetry, art, scholarship, and conversations about the body, anorexia, bulimia, perfectionism and identity. People are warmly invited to read, explore, share, contribute, and join them in the fight against negative body image.

My beliefs

Counsellors need to balance their authenticity, with restraint from giving explicit advice. If I'm asked, 'What should I do?' I might say, 'Well, let me take off my Counselling Hat, and blow the cobwebs off my Problem-Solving Hat'. I may pass on ideas that others found helpful, or I may annoyingly say, 'What advice would you give a friend with this same kind of problem?'

In fact, in the ACA Code of Ethics, it explicitly states: Counsellors do not normally give advice. (www.theaca.net.au)

One question I ask is, 'Do you believe in motivation from within, or do you believe people need to be pushed, cajoled and rewarded for progress? Or a bit of both?' I won't be able to change their beliefs, though I may offer researched, evidence-based practices such as Gottman's Emotion Coaching to inform them of other options to coercion, time-out and naughty chairs.

If asked for parenting suggestions, I recommend strong routines, regular bedtimes and warm encouragement and specific positive validation, such as 'Thanks for the help with the dishes.' I suggest avoiding reactions such as 'Look, you've left me to do the dishes again. No screen time for you tonight'.

I am not an advocate of reward charts as they are often inconsistently applied. Also, the person in charge of the stickers has too much power. If the child sets a reward book up themselves, then I'm fine with that. I am an advocate of increasing children's freedoms and responsibilities year by year.

This book has invited the reader to journey alongside me, with how I position myself as a counsellor. But this chapter is now about you. You have your own values and beliefs about how children should be supported, how parents should work together and support their growing children. What direction is your compass pointing to?

Summary

Engaging with parents is ideal. Growth and change does not happen in isolation in the therapy room. It happens between sessions when children are with those close to them. Others may notice something different about the child's sense of self. A small shift in a person's identity is palpable, and energetically this creates the butterfly effect.

Children can become aware of what is important to them through counselling dialogues and play. Understanding how power dynamics may be generating many of their life problems, and finding a philosophical perspective, can lead to them becoming agents for change, and cast a large pebble in the Pond of Life. The freedom to step in this direction is available to us all. The next story shows how sometimes we may be afraid to choose that step.

TAMAR DOLEV©

The bird and the cage

By Ana Louisa Novis© (Ana is a personal friend, and gave Kim permission to publish)

The golden cage was large and very comfortable, fulfilling every desire its inhabitants could have. Besides, it was set next to a big window, that guaranteed an airy environment and a lovely exterior view.

The bird shared his lair with his parents and a dozen little birds and the cage looked almost like a vivarium. Nonetheless, he was the only one who was born there.

Everybody in the neighbourhood knew the birds. Not only because of the beautiful songs they sang at sunset, but also because of the vibrant colours of their feathering. The kids on the street always asked to visit them.

Anxious and curious, the bird loved to explore the limits of his cage, and never kept quiet for too long at the same spot. Jumping from one perch to another, he always managed to eat more fruit than the others!

At times his restlessness caused him a lot of trouble. There was a time he pushed over his drinking fountain and the water spilled all over the floor.

From an early age he was clearly different from his cage friends. Deep in his heart, there was a flame of an adventurous spirit that was only his own. Even though he had been born and raised in captivity, he had always heard a voice inside him: 'If I have wings, I am meant to fly'.

Sadly, as time went on, he also became more like the others. After all, the cage provided him food, shelter and protection. What else could he want?

As he became older and calmer he still cherished his dream of freedom. Every day, in between the small grills of the cage, he kept watching an impressive tree which towered in front of the window and he imagined how the world would look like from its top, without grills obscuring his vision.

Resigned, he avoided thinking too much about those illusions. What were the chances he would be there one day? He accepted he was destined to spend his entire life in the same cage where he was born.

And so his life went on, until, one evening, a big storm started, with thunder and lightning coming from all sides. The window was left open and a strong wind came in, throwing the cage to the ground. Some of his companions hurt themselves badly, and he was lucky he didn't get hurt as well. With the impact, the door of the cage unlocked.

Finally, his big opportunity had come!

However, approaching the open gate, he didn't manage to move: fear paralysed him. So many times he had dreamed about escaping the cage and now the opportunity was right there, in front of him, but he couldn't move a muscle. His heart beat extremely fast. To make matters worse, in that frightful night, the world out there, that had always looked so inviting, seemed to be falling apart under heavy rain, thunders and lightnings.

Suddenly, while the wind was hissing, he had the impression of hearing a voice that whispered to him: 'Follow your heart!'

That was the little push he needed to give him courage! He crossed the threshold of the cage and flew into the room, guided by his instincts.

The noise woke up the owners of the house, who rushed in to help the poor little animals.

The following morning, everything had gotten back to normal, with only one difference. One of the birds had disappeared. After a lot of searching, the owners gave up. From that day on, there would be one less bird.

Some days later, all of them were surprised by a beautiful song coming from the big tree in front of the cage. There he was, perched on the highest branch, watching the world from the place he had always desired, greeting his beloved friends.

The wind of the frightful night brought him both agony and happiness. Since then, he would always listen to the voice of his heart whenever he had to make a decision.

After some time, that familiar restlessness came back to his heart. He knew it was time to go and step forward into the unknown.

After casting one last glance at the golden cage, he spread his wings and disappeared into the horizon.

Actions to take as a result of reading this chapter

1. Look online for an old poem by Rumi, called *The Guest House*, and reflect on your responses.

2. Research philosophers such as Heidegger or Kierkegaard, and reflect on your own beliefs about life, the development of your own identity, fate or free will, and your purpose on your relatively brief life journey.

3. If fairness and equality are values you hold dear, how do you sit with children who suffer in unfair life situations such as poverty and abuse? What role does counselling play in righting wrongs, or do you have another belief, mission or passion?

CHAPTER 11

Who's on Your Team?

> 'We are like islands in the sea, separate on the surface but connected in the deep.'
>
> **WILLIAM JAMES**

Trauma and loss can shake-up a person's sense of courage, belonging and hope. The Team of Life and Tree of Life are two key creative, expressive arts activities that are helpful once the young person or child (eight years plus) has found a safe haven in the counselling space, and after emotional support and some stability has been established.

These two techniques of narrative therapy using visual, relational metaphors have proven their usefulness in healing after trauma, by re-introducing a sense of wholeness and connection. Both draw on strength-based theories, and can be created in one, or over a few sessions, with individuals, the whole family or as group activities.

I see these two activities as capturing the person's whole wonderful self, and their chosen mob. They offer a platform to show to the world, their final push back against the impact of adversity. Children are often astonished at the richness of their identity, and one nine-year-old told me after his Tree of Life, 'There's more to me than you think!'

These exercises require no drawing skills, and although they come with prescriptive guidelines, they can be adapted by, or to suit the child.

The Team of Life

The Team of Life uses a sporting metaphor developed by David Denborough from Dulwich Centre Foundation. Discussions about team spirit in sport might be a starting point for rich conversations, with the main aim being to build a sense of having an identity that includes precious values and important people in their life.

I may ask, 'Do you think you and your family would be interested in "teaming up" and making trouble for The Problem? Maybe for the next session you could come in with Dad and Mum, and we can work on a new project: The Team of Life!'

> *'A team is not a group of people that work together.*
> *A team is a group of people that trust each other.'*
> **Simon Sinek**

A young person may follow a football team, and so grasp the challenges and benefits of working in a team towards achieving goals. A 12-year-old boy, whose circle of connections was small due to a speech problem, enjoyed using a tennis court metaphor. His sporting experience was that he played 'doubles' in tennis on the weekend with his parents and a grandmother. Another child used his online team's gaming adventures for his exploration of who and what was important for him. Dad and Mum were both listed as the referees and refreshments helpers!

This process helps to create a bond and a sense of connection between the members of their chosen 'team', and encourages young people to value the support they receive and recognise those who are, or who have been most influential in their lives.

Naming your team and what it stands for

These are the kinds of questions which can help populate the playing field with their names, drawn on a large piece of paper, or on the Zoom whiteboards.

Questions to help bring stories, connections and values to the drawing include:

- Who are the people who play an important role in your life? These people can be alive, no longer living or superheroes of any kind. Favourite players, authors, teachers or mentors. They might be people who you've known from the past. What did you learn from them?
- Who might know your life goals? Who's your goalkeeper, that reliable person who has your back, who keeps The Problem from scoring too many goals against you? These

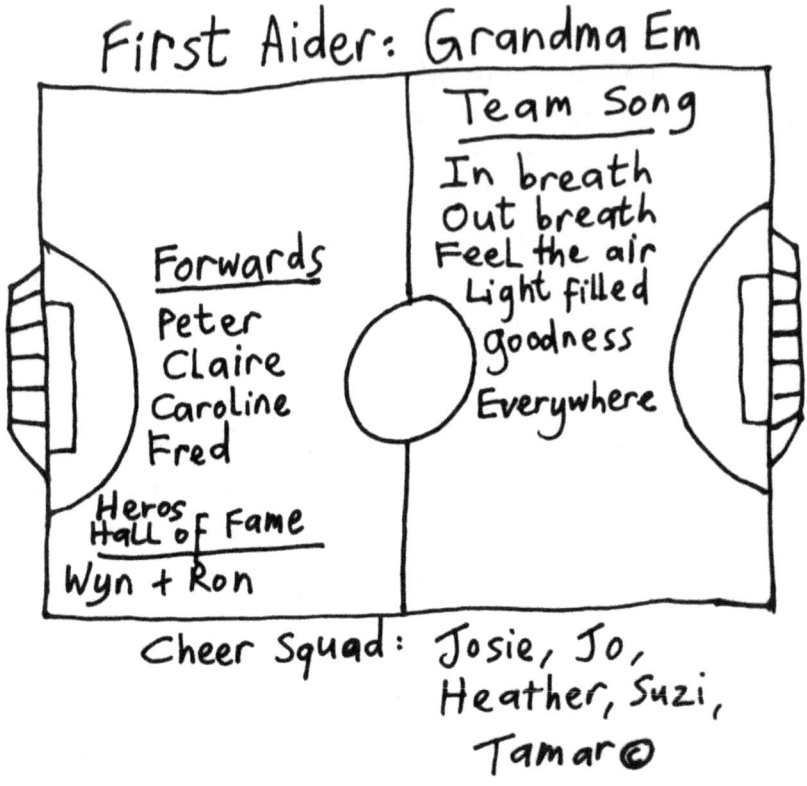

people embody the person's values of living, so we can further unpack this. What qualities do these people have and how do you see them demonstrating these in action?
- Who do you choose as coach? How do they inspire or encourage you? Why does this work for you? What are some of the things that they have taught you?
- What's the name of your home ground? I usually use the mindfulness exercise, 'Finding a precious place and a moment in time' to help the person picture this (see Chapter 5). This could be their family's home country, or a place of spiritual ancestral significance that they visit in their memories or dreams.

- What's your team mascot and team colours? Can you write a short team song, that reminds the team how to keep on carrying on? What name would you give your team?
- What has the team already achieved? How have past goals been celebrated? If there has not been a recognition of past successes, documents and medals can be created and pronounced to the wider team.
- I may step into the role of sports journalist. How have you and your team tackled the problem in the past, and what do you think are the reasons for these wins?
- Can you tell me a story about a teammate who stepped in, and ran with the ball?
- Looking back, what strengths have helped you and what skills are you using most? What have you learnt about yourself in using these against life's problems?

Tree of Life

The Tree of Life was developed over 20 years ago by psychologist Ncazelo Ncube in southern Africa, with children who had become orphans and had suffered multiple trauma and losses as a result of HIV/AIDS.

The Tree of Life can reclaim identity and preferred directions in life. It uses the visual metaphor of a tree, with each part of the tree carrying stories that represent the past, present and future. The person reconstructs their identity at each stage through responding to narrative-style questions.

Research has shown the Tree of Life can increase a sense of self and contribute to the child's ability to articulate what is important to them, and help reconnect them with others. The image of the tree further increases the child's feelings of safety and strength.

Mala German's research article (2013) about the use of Tree of Life in a school setting in London explains that it is a psychosocial strength-based intervention that is grounded in narrative practice and theory. German's research provided evidence that the tree intervention created statistically significant improvements in self-concept as measured by Becks BSCI-Y standardised scores.

I recommend reading, 'The Mighty Oak', a beautiful article written by Janelle Dickson published in *The International Journal of Narrative Therapy and Community Work* in 2009. Dickson describes using the Tree of Life method with 16-year-old, Dylan, who was experiencing bullying, and found himself engaged in anger and aggression.

The Tree of Life can be used after trauma, when clients are weighed down by their 'problem story'. When a client is struggling with symptoms such as negativity and ruminations, or finding it hard to reflect on their strengths, or value-laden hopes for the future, this technique can bring a healing perspective.

Because the tree is a metaphor for the child's problem-free identity, I recommend getting playful with colour, and not colouring the soil brown, leaves green and sky blue. Adolescents may wish to use only pencil, or ink. Younger children can paint the tree one week, and then begin writing the words the next week in texta.

How I assess for suitability

I introduce these interventions after some therapeutic work, using the kinds of approaches you can see from this book. Once I start hearing more stories of the child having influence over the problem, I can ask what is called a 're-membering' question. These invite the child to consider *who* they feel connected to, and wish to recognise, and re-enrol as members of their life journey.

'How do we know when someone is important to us? What is it about how they make us feel?' There is a story about a little boy who said 'The way someone says your name is different when they love you. You know your name is safe in their mouth.'

'So, who else knows this about you? Who else would be sitting here nodding and saying, "Oh, yes, I knew Oscar could do this, I know Oscar has what it takes"? How would they know that about you? Is there a story you could tell about what they've seen over the years?' We can help the client find out what it might mean to them to know there are people who want to be here for them, and who understand them.

I usually have a session prior to beginning the Tree of Life to assess how well the tree might work. I show the Strengths Cards® and invite the child to choose five or six and ask them to tell a story of how each are a good fit for them. A child on the autism spectrum may have difficulty grasping the concept of their strengths or the tree metaphor. In such a situation, I may create a simplified version for the following week.

With children from out-of-home care background, the roots can be confronting, and may need to be adapted to be more future-focused, such as, 'What new roots are you intending to put down for your future?' Similarly, adaptations may be needed when a young person has been struggling with depression. The soil or branches might prove a challenge, and we can instead use solution questions. 'If the depression finally packed its bags and hit the road, what can you see yourself doing each week that could regain your vitality? What hopes for the future might leap into your heart?'

When could I use this?

When a child is struggling with negativity and ruminations, or finding it hard to reflect on their strengths, or hopes for the future and may have lost touch with their values, the Tree of Life questions and images elicit different responses from the usual 'problem' story conversations.

How long does it take?

With young children, the tree can be painted in week 1, their strengths discussed and captured with vivid anecdotes in week 2, and stories to fill the rest of the tree completed in week 3. Otherwise it can be completed in one or two hours.

How to begin?

When introducing Tree of Life ideas with young people I may point out a de-identified picture made by another child on our counselling room wall. I ask if they would like to create their own tree. Then, we might go outside and find a tree, and talk about how the roots are hidden underground—every day quietly bringing goodness to the tree, like things that you've been doing that are fun. Maybe skateboarding or baking a cake with Nan?

By being with a real tree, children begin drawing on their kinaesthetic, sensory and imaginative experience of a tree ... not just an abstract concept. Even if I only have one hour, I've found that a gentle 10 minutes with a real tree is a good amount of time for connection.

Instructions for meeting a tree

Working remotely, I may send these instructions via email and when we have our next session, I can ask about the person's responses to the experience of finding and being with their tree.

1. Take in the <u>whole tree</u>. Then, close your eyes and picture the activity in the roots and soil—they bring nourishment to the tree. The roots symbolise your family ancestry and family rituals you value.

2. Reflect on how the <u>roots</u> are hidden underground—every day they quietly bring goodness from the soil to the tree.

3. Look at the <u>soil</u> and the earth closely. If you are comfortable, sit on the ground under the tree or touch the earth. We connect with the earth in a tactile sensory way, and if we are barefoot, our over-active electrical circuits will be discharged, and we will go inside more balanced. The soil represents what we do day to day. It's ever-changing, but it replenishes us.

4. Now feel the bark on the <u>trunk</u>. Can you push the tree over, or at least rock it a bit? What keeps the tree strong? What keeps you strong? A strong trunk can help us stand tall when the storms arrive.

5. Look up at the <u>branches</u> overhead. They represent the future. Where might you be heading? What might you want to be doing? Is it still a little way off? Or are there some lower branches that are nearly in reach now? What aspirations and hopes for the future are you connecting with now?

6. Look at the <u>leaves</u>. There may be a few precious people (or pets) you are connected to ... and no two are alike. These are like the leaves on your tree. Can you find two leaves exactly the same? The leaves represent the beautiful relationships you have, and even if the person has died, they can still be part of your Tree of Life.

People can be invited to find something on the ground before they return to a table to begin the drawing. A piece of bark or a leaf next to them can be a tactile, sensory connection to their tree. I've also sometimes offered craft glue and scissors, and other materials for those who enjoy creating tactile art.

I might ask a child to give their tree a name, and picture it growing strong. Where is it? Near a river or mountain? We may do a guided imagery and sit under it, or climb its branches using 'A moment in time' (https://youtu.be/_ECyl75aA7k).

The resulting artwork is enjoyable to draw, and is a concrete and beautiful gathering of achievements, skills, knowledges, values and cherished hopes for the future. It supports re-membering connections with important people in our lives and can be a springboard for identity renewals. I remind children to put the date on the reverse side.

In a group setting, a forest of trees can be created at the end, and I encourage those interested to read more from the Dulwich Centre's website. I have photos of each tree part with the guiding prompts (see below) on a laminated sheet for in-person work. I also let things evolve freely according to people's imaginations. There is a four-line song I introduce, which can also be sung as a round, 'Trees Grow Tall in the Heart of the Forest' (https://youtu.be/94zHVAfGuFE).

Parts of the tree

1. Roots: where I come from
The 'roots' provide an opportunity to reflect and share stories about significant people who've contributed to a person's life. Michael White found that voices from a person's life, past and present, are influential in the construction of a person's identity.

What fond memories do you have of time spent with your family? What is the significance of your family name, your own name and ancestry? This may include extended family, or those who have passed away:

- Who has taught you important life lessons and skills in your life?
- What is your favourite home/family song/dance or other activity?
- What foods are special? Why?
- Do you have any family mottos or sayings?
- Are there links from these valued family pearls to your own strengths (in the trunk)?

2. The ground: what sustains you?

This may contribute to helping find a 'safe place' from which to be and reflect. Questions are oriented in the present situation:

- Where do you live now?
- What activities are you engaged in with your daily life, hobbies, self-care, sports, etc.?

There is often a link between each part of the tree:

- Who have you modelled your daily activities from?
- Could that person be acknowledged in the roots?

3. Strengths: a strong trunk

The 'trunk' conversations bring forth creative abilities, interests, skills, and strengths. This contributes to building self-esteem. The trunk helps people internalise their strengths and abilities. A 'positive identity' conclusion is being developed, shared and witnessed. Other metaphors can then build on the experience, such as, 'Year by year, our wisdom grows—like the rings inside the tree trunk'.

- Tell a story about one of these Strength Cards® (or use a list of strengths)
- What does this strength look like in your life?
- Why it is important to you?
- When did you start practising this strength/skill?
- Tell a story of your earliest memory using this strength in your life
- Who might you have been learning this from?
- What would they say, if they were privy to this conversation?

4. The branches: hopes for the future

Branches encourage some really imaginative 'dream talk' which can enable people to have space to think about their ideas, long forgotten wishes and dreams for the future. This can create increased motivation in the present, and again, can be linked to other parts of the tree using re-membering conversations:

- Who might have shared such hopes with you when you were a young person?
- Who knows you have been holding this cherished wish in your heart?
- How long have you had these hopes and dreams?
- How are these linked to significant people in your life?
- How have you managed to hold on to these dreams?
- What has sustained your hopes?

5. The leaves: important people in your life

The 'leaves' of the tree represent people or pets who are important. They can be people who may be alive or have passed on. Just because people are no longer alive, it does not mean they are not still very important to us.

People you value or hold precious in your life 'make your heart warm'. They may be fictional characters who inspired you, or family pets who helped you through hard times.

- Why are these people special to you?
- Did you have a lovely time with this person?
- What was special about this person to you?
- Would this person like it that you remember them in these ways?
- How might your presence in their life have contributed to their happiness?

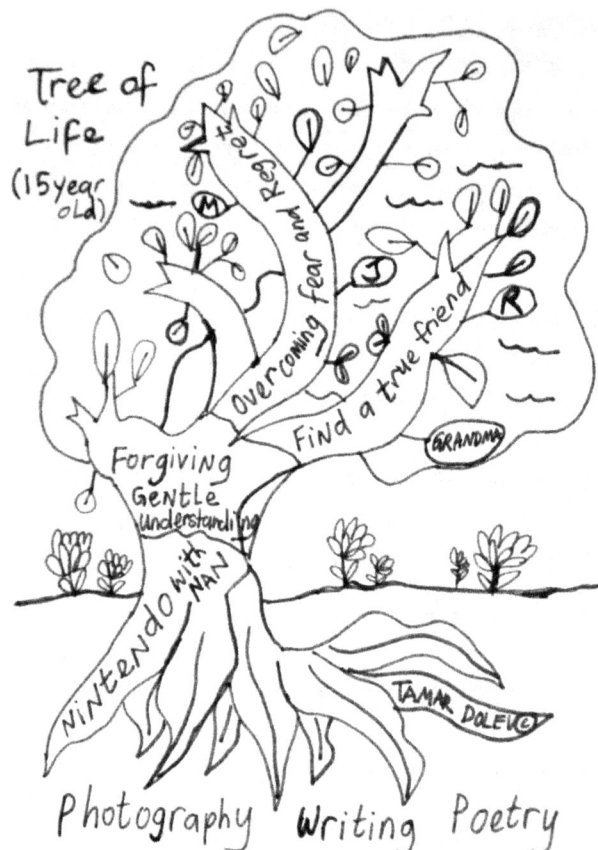

Staying safe

With older children, a compost bin is sometimes drawn to hold the fallen leaves. This may represent people who've been, or are in their lives still, but who compromise the child's safety or wellbeing. However, perhaps that person will see their leaf is missing! That might make things worse. We have other ways to resist the need to include people in a child's tree equally.

Children may sometimes draw a leaf just about to fall, with a teeny-tiny gap between the leaf and the branch. Others make the leaf smaller, or use a colour that is a muddy colour. These are subtle acts of resistance, and help the child have agency over who they value. I may even introduce the Mary Poppins video clip at this point!

Summary of the two methods

As well as being foundational gems from the narrative treasure cave, these healing activities can help clients move through times of feeling stuck. They are future oriented and positive.

When a child has been impacted adversely through trauma and loss, starved of the joy of 'belonging,' feeling powerless, isolated or in despair, these activities offer safe and fertile grounds for the development of alternative stories of strength, connection, hope and self-compassion.

They can be helpful to bring the therapeutic work to a satisfying close. They are strength-based, and from this position, they can support the young person to stand strong in their future-building.

Actions to take as a result of reading this chapter

1. Book into one of the many training opportunities to learn more about the Tree of Life.

2. Check out the Dulwich Centre website for additional resources.

3. Create your own Tree or Team of Life.

CHAPTER 12

Saying Goodbye

The final stage of counselling is a time to pause and reflect on what has been achieved. Wisdom can be gathered and plans can be formed for ways a young person might stay connected with their strengths, values, hopes and dreams.

Sometimes our child clients find it painful to break that attachment bond to their special person and place. I have a box of crystals, and children can choose one to take home on their last session. This is a symbolic, 'transitional object'. I may also send a letter of closure to the child.

I often tell this story, *The Queen, the Crown and the Storyteller*, which describes the mayhem of earlier days, and how in the stillness and safety of the counselling space, ways forward have become visible.

I also email a link to the story, recorded for them to play later (https://youtu.be/-d2T_FDZv40).

The Queen, the Crown and the Storyteller

Warriors and statesmen alike looked down on the Queen's storyteller, a mere harlequin-coated entertainer, telling worthless tales of idle fantasy.

One day the Queen was leaning over a pool in the palace gardens when the crown fell from her head and sank without trace, despite her frantic attempts to grab it.

Warrior after warrior dived in to get it; ministers fished with net and line all to no avail.

Queen and court were in a desperate panic—until the storyteller stood up and told a powerful and fascinating story of crowns and jewels, and the finding of secret treasures.

They all fell under the spell of the tale, and were very quiet as he concluded.

Then, to their amazement, he leapt nimbly into the water and emerged seconds later with the crown—which he had been able to see easily now that the waters were undisturbed and still.

Parkinson, R. (2009). *Transforming tales: How stories can change people.* Jessica Kingsley Publications.
Reproduced with permission of the Licensor through PLSclear.

Our small clients are the ones who will soon graduate from The School of Life: 101-Childhood. After counselling, children may be more able to tell their story in ways that make them stronger. Our role includes walking beside and bearing witness to their emerging identity, as they understand their personal values and skills (identified through creative, playful activities, and interesting dialogues) so children and young people can step into life from a new position.

Their CV includes their skills in knowing how problems sneak into families (Chapters 3 & 4), and the way emotions emerge, and how feelings can quickly escalate, becoming potentially harmful (Chapters 5 & 6).

Some may have developed an understanding of and been able to begin adapting to the unfairness of loss (Chapter 7), how power plays out in their life (Chapter 9), and see that 'life is a journey' (Chapter 8).

Children are often willing to share their tips and ideas with others that come after them. Children can be invited to contribute their 'know-how about getting through hard times' to a Virtual Art Gallery, or Wisdom Book (de-identified and with consent). This is a coffee table style of book, similar to the type you may write in after a stay at a holiday accommodation. Some create their own lucky-dip jar to take home.

One 13-year-old who had experienced bullying at his new high school wrote in the wisdom book for sharing his self-talk rebuffs: *'Yeah, right! Get over it. Yeah, so what. Don't jinx yourself'.*

Therapeutic documents

Letters written to the child by the counsellor follow a long tradition of narrative practice. (Epston, 2020) This is where the child's hard work of talking about difficult feelings and experiences, and what the counsellor has witnessed can be summed up and acknowledged formally, if it is safe to have such details in writing.

As counselling concludes, I may ask a parent if it's okay to send a letter of closure to their child, summing up their strengths and successes, and sending them good wishes for their future journey. I point out there would be no charge, but that it can sometimes be a helpful way of recognising the hard work and carrying forward the child's learnings, achievements and intentions.

Sometimes, a child wants to write their own letter. I still well-up recalling Josh, aged four-and-a-half, who spoke while I wrote on some paper:

> *'Dear Josh. When you are five and at school, remember to do your homework. You will be playing chess, and at first you may not do very well, but with practice you will get better. You will be playing AFL, soccer and basketball. You will be playing well. From Josh.'*

Measuring outcomes

Single session frameworks allow for us to check-in every session, as if it was to be our last. 'How are we going today? Are we talking about the things you were hoping we'd get to, or is there something else that you've noticed may be worth talking about?' We can find ways to ask what the counselling experience is like for the child, and what they think might be more useful.

Measuring outcomes can be an agency requirement, but also it's good practice to have some way of getting feedback about what a young person found helpful, what was not so helpful, what might be good to do or talk about next session, and what they might have learnt that felt important to them, to carry forwards. I include these as casual, yet regular conversations at the end of each session, and sometimes formalised into an outcome chart where the person can tick a box, or if they are young, draw a face.

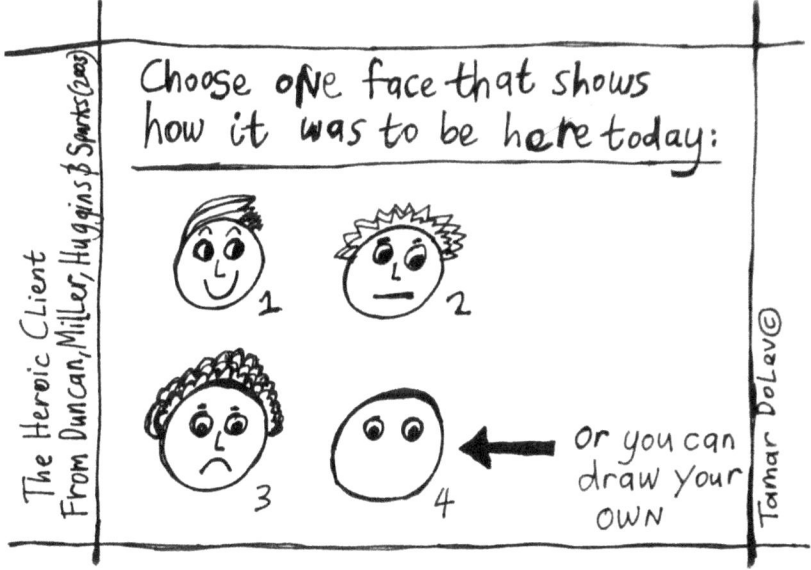

Some other ways to gain feedback:

- Can you point to anything helpful or interesting from our time together? Could you give the helpfulness of today's session a score out of 10?

- Can you put on this line ☹ _____ ☺ how you're feeling we went today? (adapted from The Heroic Client 'Outcome Scaling Chart', Duncan, Miller & Sparks).
- Could you tell me something that was irritating, or not helpful about the session today? Your feedback is useful to me, as I get to see other children and I can always improve what kind of things I do, so go for it!
- Is there one small thing you're thinking you might do a bit differently after today? Are you seeing the problem in a new way? Would it be helpful for me to write these things down for you to take home, or would you like to, or can you remember them?
- I see other children with tricky problems. Have you got any good tips to help other children with similar problems? You could write them in the Wisdom Book.
- Is there anyone you would like me to speak to, about things we talked about today? Or would you like most of it, or all of it to stay private? As I mentioned at the beginning, if I was worried about safety, I would need to talk to someone. (If needed: There was one thing you said that I want to check with you ...)

Family meetings

Parents may fear that after counselling, things may drift backwards. A return to counselling might represent to them a 'failure,' so we can suggest something that might fit with the family's level of willingness and capacities to keep up with the collaborative approach they were part of in counselling.

I recommend family meetings, which work well with children from about four years old. They are opportunities for parents and children to celebrate successes and hear what others think about important issues. I ask parents, 'What do you want your home to look like, feel like, sound like? What rituals might you create together? Would problems find it hard to get a foot in the door if they had to face the whole family teaming up together?'

Family meetings can bring fun to the family tasks of problem-solving, as well as strengthening communication and nurturing positive relationships. They can be exciting events where families can plan, create and spend quality times together, and catch up on what's going on for everyone. They are safe places to talk about, and prepare everyone for changes to family life, such as divorce, a recently diagnosed illness or a new baby. They are not just a place to air grievances.

I suggest parents simply buy a cheap school exercise book and write on the cover: *The Solution Book*. (Because magically, if anyone writes a 'problem' into it, when the book is opened as a group for discussion, then solutions appear!)

I say, 'Leave this on top of the fridge, and anyone, anytime can write a problem or a request in it, with their name and date. Then once a week, 30 minutes can be allocated to sit together as a family. A pot of tea can be prepared, or a special homemade dessert can be shared. Everyone can take turns to chair the meetings, keeping the mood light, but also serious, as topics are discussed. Any solutions found can be documented (and importantly) include a review date set in a months' time.

Several documented outcomes of such practices include: learning about each other (curiosity), developing communication skills (sociability), collaboratively overcoming challenges (resilience), finding ways to reflect on feelings (self-awareness), discussing values (integrity), setting shared goals (resourcefulness), finding pleasure creating ways to inspire one another (creativity), and fostering gratitude, appreciation and understanding (empathy).

In the *New York Times* Bestseller, *The Secrets of Happy Families*, Bruce Felier incorporated a weekly 'review and retrospective' into his family meetings that included these questions:

1. What worked well in our family this week?
2. What went wrong in our family this week?
3. What will we work on this coming week?

Appreciations can become part of an opening ritual. Each family member can acknowledge things they've noticed this week about other members. This may include a thank you for baking cookies, congratulations on a project, or a kind word about something nice that a person did. Adults can also use these opportunities to model apologising when they step outside of their values.

The last meeting

We now handover to the whole family. You may like to create your own ritual, but if I began working with a family with the 'Tea Party' (Chapter 1) I invite everyone to a farewell tea party, and send invitations.

At that last meeting, I may ask 'What might be helpful next? Do you think you and your family are interested in "teaming up" and being the goalkeepers, making trouble for the problem to make sure it doesn't get back in the lead?'

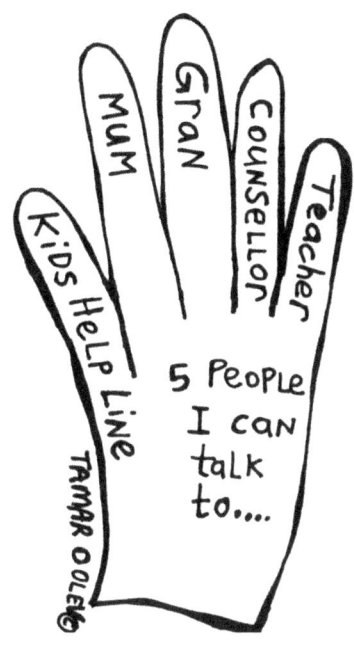

I will check-in, 'If you discover a new problem, or wanted to talk with someone about troubles, who are the people you'll feel most comfortable to talk to? Can you make a list or draw around your hand, and in each finger put a name? What about putting Kids Helpline in your thumb?'

This might include showing how a feedback chart for the whole family works, using a calendar. I suggest that each month, at a family meeting, a new whole-family goal is chosen. It may be as simple as everyone contributed that day to making dinner or clearing up after dinner. One family chose random acts of kindness. The family can apply stickers to the days they reach that peak in achievement.

Summary

Preparing for the last session and tuning in to how the child and family may feel is part of our job. Every year we experience dozens of farewells which are all breaks in the therapeutic alliance/attachments we make. We are not a village, so it is quite likely the child will never see us again. We will never forget each other.

Writing a letter or having a special treasure chest with crystals for a child to choose one from to take home may be a hugely significant act. I have a virtual wisdom jar my online clients can add to. Children have so many unique ideas of what has helped them, and they like to share these with others that come after them: paying it forward.

In the narrative tradition, we also say how working with the family has helped us grow, A goodbye ritual of some kind always feels appropriate. What might yours be?

As counsellors, we need to find ways that keep us connected to our wiser self. For me, this story represents how I picture my work as a counsellor, and the reality of my role.

The Starfish Story
originally written by Loren Eiseley in 1969

One day a man was walking along the beach when he noticed a boy picking something up and gently throwing it into the ocean.

Approaching the boy, he asked, 'What are you doing?'

The boy replied, 'Throwing starfish back into the ocean. The surf's up and the tide is going out. If I don't throw them back, they'll die'.

The man said, 'Don't you realise there are miles and miles of beach, and hundreds of starfish? You can't make a difference!'

The boy stooped down and picked up another. He threw it into the ocean, and said, 'It's making a difference to this one'.

Actions to take as a result of reading this chapter

1. Write a letter to a child client that you have been recently working with. Reflect on what they, and you, have been learning.

2. Research some child-friendly outcome measures that fit with your preferred ways of working.

3. Put some thought to a ritual you can create for your last session.

APPENDIX 1

Safety First

As a counsellor, I picture us having a few metaphoric life jackets. Should there be a disclosure of harm, we need to be prepared and don our own jacket swiftly, and offer the other to our client. As we gently tread water beside the client, we can breathe slowly and deeply, and ask 'What might help keep you safer? Let's create a safety plan which will include who will be in your survival craft'.

Confidentiality

As soon as possible in the first session, we need to explain the boundaries of confidentiality:

'When we talk about things in this counselling space, they are private ... between us, unless I'm worried someone might be getting hurt, or if someone is not safe. That's my job—to help people find ways to understand their lives a bit more, to see if we can come up with ways to shrink problems and to feel safer and stronger.

If I'm worried about your safety, or the safety of someone else, then I could not just let you leave and not do anything. If a friend was not safe, you would also want to take some action. I would try and change things, but I would speak with you first and ask if you had any ideas or worries about who else might need to know. So sometimes, what we talk about might not be so private. Do you understand that?'

Should the case be heading to court or have Child Protection involvement, then the child needs to know that. 'What we write down can sometimes be seen by a judge who can make decisions to protect children and families. Judges are very careful about who else gets to know about things we talk about. You can ask me any questions about this.' In such cases, counsellors need to be aware that there is a very high likelihood of their case notes being subpoenaed.

Duty of care to protect children

Counsellors make assessments and respond to risk according to their statutory and ethical obligations, which are to protect the wellbeing of children, families and ourselves as we carry out our valuable work. Practitioners need to be alert for symptoms and indications of abuse and self-harm and be prepared to respond protectively.

Children's safety and wellbeing must be central to all our work. During the course of any counselling session, groupwork or consultation with parents or teachers, there may be an indication that a child has been abused, is currently at risk, or it is reasonably believed the child could be at future risk from abuse, neglect or harm.

There can be a need for a child protection notification, police welfare check, a crisis response intervention, or a specialist referral such as to CASA. We must be ready for such a time, and have the relevant contact numbers on hand. Working remotely, you will need to ensure you know the address of the young person, in case there is a need for a police welfare check in a different state.

Responding to self-harm and risk

When I come across a possible high-risk situation and I must ask the child about a safety matter, I may say, 'I need to take off my counselling hat, and put on my safety hat for a few minutes'.

I may have already been administering the versatile K10 self-assessment tool with 14-year-olds and upwards (found on the Beyondblue website: https://www.beyondblue.org.au/the-facts/anxiety-and-depression-checklist-k10) to get a sense for their wellbeing. This is accessible from their phone, and monthly check-ins can attend to any trends. The online score of the impact of stress reveals a low, medium or high range, and provides a prompt for what to do next.

With new clients who are not yet sensing that therapeutic trust has been developed, I may show this versatile 'matrix of truth' below. It invites the young person to think for themselves and take some ownership and responsibility for what is really going on.

Is your 'I dunno' reply a code for:

1. I really have no idea
2. I know, but I don't want to talk today
3. I don't know, and don't care to know right now
4. I don't know and I'm open to exploring this.

These same responses can be used around family violence at home: 'What are your thoughts on your dad choosing to abuse you and hit you with a spoon?' or 'Is there something that's happened that has drawn you back into self-harm?' or 'Do you know why your teacher asked you to stop by today?'

When discussing suicide, I may use a question from Irvin Yalom's book *The Gift of Therapy*. 'Some part of you has brought the rest of you here today. Could I speak with the part of you that wants to live?' I also ask, 'What are the codes we can use at our check-in time of the session? Red could let me know you have a plan and are thinking about taking that final step. Orange can be when you are thinking about this every day but resisting taking the next step. Green can be you're confident that although the thoughts come and go, you feel certain you would not kill yourself'.

Ensuring you receive supervision in such cases is essential. A safety plan for your client, including calling helplines and a family or friend, as well as 'How will you know it's time to activate your safety plan?' discussions are needed.

An article I wrote for *Counselling Australia Journal*, titled 'Twenty new conversations about suicide' provides further tips and strategies for talking about this important subject. (https://www.theaca.net.au/journals/ACAMagVol21No3.pdf).

We need to educate the young people about our mandatory requirements to notify others when there is a risk of harm, or disclosure of historical abuse. 'Who would you prefer I talk to, Mum or Dad first?' is a well-worn phrase that lets children know we don't keep something secret when safety is involved, and neither should they. 'If your friend came and said, "I'm going to kill myself tonight. Please don't tell anyone," what would you do? What is the right thing to do, the ethical thing to do?'

I have also created this CHANGE acronym prompt to start conversations about personal agency. I invite some storytelling about small changes they may have implemented or noticed in the week. It becomes part of our familiar risk-assessment point in the session, the same way a doctor routinely measures a patient's blood pressure. We can write it on the Zoom whiteboard, or in session on paper:

CHANGE:
Care for self
Hate towards self
Anger at others
Nice to others
Growth
Enjoyment

I would suggest all counsellors check the Australian Kids Helpline website for ways to talk with young people about thoughts about ending their lives and self-harm. There are excellent videos and 24/7 webchat and email counselling support in addition to the phoneline. Parents can be introduced to this too: https://kidshelpline.com.au/teens/issues/self-harm.

Family Violence

Family violence is when a person chooses to abuse another, often based on the belief that they are entitled to power and control to the point that they disregard the feelings of their partner and/or children.

Child counsellors need to take extreme care with their note taking, because working with children around separation and family violence, intervention orders, Family Court matters and such can result in their files being subpoenaed. Child counsellors must ask every parent at intake to see all IVOs and Family Court orders, because even seeing a child for one session may contravene a court order which says both parents need to agree to child counselling.

Counsellors working from a home therapy room also need to be vigilant around not having their home address on any form of media, and plan for the worst: a woman's phone may be being tracked, or there could be a listening and/or tracking device in a child's toy.

Specialist support services

Specialist support services for children and their families who have experienced abuse exist throughout Australia. Your local Child Protection Agency will be able to provide details of appropriate services and support. Contact details for these agencies are detailed here: http://www.aihw.gov.au/child-protection/.

The Australian Institute of Family Studies (AIFS) have produced a comprehensive practice brief on responding to children and young people's disclosures of abuse with clear advice for both professionals and family or friends: http://www.aifs.gov.au/nch/pubs/brief/pb2/pb2.pdf.

Indigenous children and families

When an Indigenous child or adolescent experiences trauma, loss or grief, there can be extra complexities that need to be taken into account. Aboriginal and Torres Strait Islander Australians' experiences of loss are multifaceted and complex, and involve the 'normal' losses that people experience as well as the other losses that are specific to Indigenous Australians.

Aboriginal and Torres Strait Islander Australians have historical and cultural ways of dealing with loss. These differences should be considered, however, being culturally sensitive should be balanced with best practice principles. The Australian Child and Adolescent Trauma, Loss and Grief Network has some useful resources on their website: https://earlytraumagrief.anu.edu.au/resource-centre/indigenous-children-families

Supervision

Supervision is my safe haven. Consultation with a supervisor can be a time to reflect about your cases, your self-care, and what competencies you may wish to further develop to best carry your caseload. Workplaces may have a tiered management system to support a counsellor, but independent practitioners would need to contact their clinical supervisor to discuss any concerns around client risk and reporting. As such, practitioners must have a clear understanding of their legal and ethical obligations, in particular around 'mandatory reporting' requirements under their state Family Law Act.

I have needed to seek additional supervision to respond to the intensity of transference-countertransference dynamics with children and young people, who have experienced complex trauma. To avoid burnout, you may need that extra pair of ears and a trusted connection with your supervisor.

APPENDIX 2

Summary of Narrative Therapy

Narrative approaches keep counsellors curious, and invite the client to think about things they have not previously considered: what's important to them and what's worked in the past. A sacred space is created for reflection and listening to what the inner voice is saying. Identity is being shaped and preferred directions recalibrated through every story told.

A summary of key narrative tools includes exploring:

1. Externalising the problem – add 'The' in front of the word and point to the problem together.
2. History of the problem – draw a timeline or graph. 'How long have you been noticing this problem? What effect does the problem have on your life?'

3. Scaling the problem – 'Is this a big, middle sized or small problem?'
4. Strengths and skills – 'Which of these have been helpful in reducing the impact of the problem, and helping you gain some ground back from the problem?'
5. Values – 'Why is this problem not so good? How would you prefer things to be? Why is that important to you? How long have you held these values as precious?'
6. Re-membering – 'Who would understand that about you? What story might they share about how your resistance to The Problem would be no surprise to them?'
7. Unique outcomes/sparkling moments – 'What were you doing when you last got some more space from The Problem? How did you achieve that? What else might be possible to do to arrange another score against The Problem's influence in your life?'
8. Re-authoring – 'What might it look like if you got to stay close to your values and strengths moving forwards? What would that mean to you and make possible, to stand firm by what you believe?'

References

Books

Axline, V. (1990). *Dibs in search of self* (reprint). Random House USA.

Bettelheim, B. (1984). *The uses of enchantment: The meaning and importance of fairy tales.* Knopf.

Billington, K. (2014, August 4–8). *Story medicine with children: Using stories after trauma to engage children and facilitate healing.* [Conference presentation]. 2014 Childhood Trauma Conference, Melbourne, Australia.

Campbell, J. (1968). *The hero with a thousand faces.* Princeton University Press.

Carey, L. (2010). Family genograms using miniature objects. In L. Lowenstein (Ed.), *Creative family therapy techniques* (pp. 20–22). Champion Press.

Denborough, D. (2008). *Collective narrative practice: Responding to individuals, groups and communities who have experienced trauma.* Dulwich Centre Publications.

Dickson, J. (2009). The 'mighty oak': Using the 'Tree of Life' methodology as a gateway to the other maps of narrative practice. *The International Journal of Narrative Therapy and Community Work, 4*, 9–23.

Doctor, P & Del Carmen, R. (Directors). (2015). *Inside Out.* Pixar Animation Studios; Walt Disney Pictures.

Duncan, B.L., Miller, S.D. & Sparks, J.A. (2004). *The heroic client: A revolutionary way to improve effectiveness through client-directed, outcome-informed therapy.* Jossey-Bass.

Engel, S. (2005). The narrative worlds of what is and what if. *Cognitive Psychology 20*, 514–525.

Epston, D. (1992). Temper tantrum parties: Saving face, losing face or going off your face. In D. Epston & M. White, *Experience, contradiction, narrative and imagination.* (pp. 37–74). Dulwich Centre Publications.

Epston, D. (2008). Taming the terrier. In *Down under and up over: Travels with narrative therapy* (pp. 73–80). Association of Family Therapy.

Felier, B. (2013) *The secrets of happy families: Improve your mornings, rethink family dinner, fight smarter, go out and play – and much more.* Little, Brown Book Group.

Fredman, G. (2018). *Death talk: Conversations with children and families.* Routledge.

Freeman, J., Epston, D. & Lobovits, D. (1997). *Playful approaches to serious problems: Narrative therapy with children and their families.* W.W. Norton & Co.

Gendlin, E. T. (2003) *Focusing: how to gain direct access to your body's knowledge.* Vintage Publishing.

German, M. (2013) Developing our cultural strengths: Using the 'Tree of Life' strength-based, narrative therapy intervention in schools, to enhance self-esteem, cultural understanding and to challenge racism. *Educational & Child Psychology, 30*(4), 75–99.

Goodman, T. A. (2005). Working with children: Beginner's mind. In Germer, C.K., Siegel, R.D. & Fulton, P.R. (Eds), *Mindfulness and psychotherapy.* Guilford Press.

Gottman, J. & Declaire, J. (1998) *Raising an emotionally intelligent child.* Prentice Hall.

Jenkins, A. (2009). *Becoming ethical.* Russell House Publishing.

Marsten, D., Epston, D. & Markham, L. (2016). *Narrative therapy in wonderland: Connecting with children's imaginative know-how.* W.W. Norton & Co.

Martin, J. (2001). *Lionheart.* Allen & Unwin.

Mehl-Madrona, M.D. & Mainguy, B. (2015). *Remapping your mind: The neuroscience of self-transformation through story.* Bear & Company.

Mehl-Madrona, L. (2005) *Coyote wisdom: the power of story in healing.* Bear & Company.

Morgan, A. (1999). Practice notes: Introducing narrative ways of working. In Dulwich Centre Publications (Ed), *Extending narrative therapy.* Dulwich Centre Publications.

Ncube, N. (2006). The Tree of Life project: Using narrative ideas in work with vulnerable children in Southern Africa. *The International Journal of Narrative Therapy and Community Work, 1*, 3–16.

REFERENCES

NHK Japan. (2015). Sleepyhead Taro and the children. In NHK Japan (Ed.), *Once upon a time in Japan* (translated by Pulvers & Carpenter). Tuttle Publishing.

Parkinson, R. (2009). *Transforming tales: How stories can change people*. Jessica Kingsley Publications.

Reynolds Roome, D. (2003). *The elephant's pillow*. Farrar Straus Giroux.

Rosen, S. (1982). *My voice will go with you: The teaching tales of Milton H. Erikson*. W.W. Norton & Co.

Rothschild, B. (2010). *8 Keys to safe trauma recovery: Take-charge strategies to empower your healing*. W.W. Norton & Co.

Seigel, D. J. & Hartzell, M. (2003). *Parenting from the inside out*. Penguin Putnam Inc.

Van Der Kolk, B. (2014) *The body keeps the score*. Penguin Books.

White, M. (2007). *Maps of narrative practice*. W.W. Norton & Co.

White, M. & Epston, D. (1990). *Narrative means to therapeutic ends*. W.W. Norton & Co.

White, M. & Morgan, A. (2006). *Narrative therapy with children and their families*. Dulwich Centre Publications.

White, M. (2000). *Reflections on narrative practice: Essays and interviews*. Dulwich Centre Publications.

White, M. (1998). Saying hullo again: The incorporation of the lost relationship in the resolution of grief. In White, C. & Denborough, D (Eds.), *Introducing narrative therapy: A collection of practice-based writings*. Dulwich Centre Publications

White, M. (2005) Children, trauma and subordinate storyline development. *The International Journal of Narrative Therapy and Community Work, 3 & 4*.

White, M. (1984). Sneaky poo. *Family Systems Medicine, 2*(2).

Yalom, I. (2017). *The gift of therapy*. Harper Collins Publishers.

Websites

Australian Child and Adolescent Trauma, Loss and Grief Network. (2020, November 24). *Bullying*. https://earlytraumagrief.anu.edu.au/resource-centre/bullying.

Australian Child and Adolescent Trauma, Loss and Grief Network. (2020, November 25). *Indigenous children and families*. https://earlytraumagrief.anu.edu.au/resource-centre/indigenous-children-families.

Australian Child and Adolescent Trauma, Loss and Grief Network. (2020, November 24). *Resource centre*. https://earlytraumagrief.anu.edu.au/resource-centre.

Australian Counselling Association. (2020). Code of Ethics and Practice of the Association for Counsellors in Australia. www.theaca.net.au.

Berry Street. (2020). *Therapeutic Life Story Work*. https://www.berrystreet.org.au/therapeutic-life-story-work.

Beyond Blue. (2020). *Anxiety and depression checklist (K10)*. https://www.beyondblue.org.au/the-facts/anxiety-and-depression-checklist-k10.

Billington, K. (2020) *Counselling Conversations*. https://www.kimbillington.com.au

Department of Health and Human Services. (2018, February 1). *What is family violence?*. https://services.dhhs.vic.gov.au/what-family-violence.

Desautels, L & McKnight, M. (2020) *Keep calm and co-regulate*. Jump Up Therapy. https://www.jumpupforkids.com.au/keep-calm-and-co-regulate/.

Dulwich Centre. (2020). *The tree of life*. https://dulwichcentre.com.au/the-tree-of-life/.

Dulwich Centre. (2007). *Externalising conversations*. https://dulwichcentre.com.au/wp-content/uploads/2019/10/Externalizing_conversations_Michael_White.pdf.

Epston, D. (2012). An emergency response to 'going off your face' at school. *Explorations: An e-journal of narrative practice, 1*. https://dulwichcentre.com.au/explorations-2012-1-david-epston.pdf.

Epston, D. (2020). *Letter-writing*. Re-Authoring Teaching. https://reauthoringteaching.com/about/what-is-narrative-therapy/david-epston-overview/david-epston-letter-writing/.

Hughes, D. (2020). What is meant by PACE? DDP Network. https://ddpnetwork.org/about-ddp/meant-pace/.

Innovative Resources. (2020). https://innovativeresources.org/.

Mehl-Madrona, L. (2020) Lewis Mehl-Madrona: Family and geriatric medicine, general psychiatry and neuropsychology. https://www.mehl-madrona.com/.

Narrative Approaches. (2020). Narrative Therapy Archive. http://www.narrativeapproaches.com/resources/narrative-therapy-archive/.

REFERENCES

Rutledge, P. (2011, January 16). *The psychological power of storytelling*. Psychology Today. https://www.psychologytoday.com/us/blog/positively-media/201101/the-psychological-power-storytelling.

Pollard, E. (2020, October 12). *Mother of bullied Indigenous boy Quaden Bayles calls for new law to address bullying at schools*. ABC News. https://www.abc.net.au/news/2020-10-12/qld-quaden-bayles-disability-royal-commission-bullying-law-call/12753862.

Price-Mitchell, M. (2019, February 14) *Family Meetings can be fun, productive and meaningful*. Roots of Action. https://www.rootsofaction.com/family-meetings/.

Raising Children Network. (2020). https://raisingchildren.net.au/.

Rock and Water. (2020) Rock and water program Gadaka Institute. https://www.rockandwater.com.au/.

Sydney Centre for Creative Change. (2020). https://www.artandplaytherapytraining.com.au/.

Tuning in to Kids. (2020). https://tuningintokids.org.au/.

White, M. (2020) Saying hullo again: The incorporation of the lost relationship in the resolution of grief. Dulwich Centre. https://dulwichcentre.com.au/product/saying-hullo-again-the-incorporation-of-the-lost-relationship-in-the-resolution-of-grief-michael-white/.

Whitney, D. (2018, July 8). The science of tears. Psych Central. https://psychcentral.com/blog/the-science-of-tears/.

Young, K. (2019). *Anxiety in teens – How to help a teenager deal with anxiety*. Hey Sigmund. https://www.heysigmund.com/anxiety-in-teens/

YouTube

Billington, K. (n.d.) Kim Billington. [YouTube channel]. Retrieved December 9, 2020, from https://www.youtube.com/channel/UCmwiHMh9DLbR2bYlpIOKqXQ/featured

Billington, K. (2020, May 10). *A moment in time*. [Video]. YouTube. https://youtube/_ECyl75aA7k

Billington, K. (2020, April 4). *The queen, the crown and the storyteller*. [Video]. YouTube. https://youtu.be/-d2T_FDZv40

Billington, K. (2020, March 21). *Trees grow tall*. [Video]. YouTube. https://youtu.be/94zHVAfGuFE

Borges, P. (2019, May 14) Gabor Maté – Authenticity vs. attachment. [Video]. YouTube. https://youtu.be/l3bynimi8HQ

Jon Harris. (2020, June 22). *Spiral drawing #388/Practice curves 3D pattern/Satisfying line illusion/Daily art therapy.* [Video]. YouTube. https://youtu.be/sMHp-yiorDE

HumanWindow. (2019, June 16). What the real cause of your anxiety is and what to do about it. Dr Gabor Maté. [Video]. YouTube. https://youtu.be/39RyGEVRbWk

Kolts, R. (2015, September 28) *Anger, compassion and what it means to be strong.* [Video]. TEDxOlympia. https://www.youtube.com/watch?v=QG4Z185MBJE

Rebel Shoes Productions. (2015, March 13) Starfish story (aka The star thrower). [Video]. YouTube. https://youtu.be/Z-aVMdJ3Aok

Salzman, J.B. & Salzman, J. (2015, January 26) Just Breathe. Wavecrest Films. [Video]. YouTube. https://youtu.be/RVA2N6tX2cg

Schwarzenegger, A. (2020, August 12). Arnold Schwarzenegger leaves the audience SPEECHLESS: One of the best motivational speeches ever. [Video]. YouTube. https://youtu.be/1bumPyvzCyo

#TheExpertLeague. (2020, May 12) Week 6 with Kim Billington. [Video] YouTube. https://youtu.be/jaVxSNVGo80

Therapy in a Nutshell. (2020, June 10). The SIFT technique for Emotion Processing: Dr. Daniel Siegel The Whole Brain Child. [Video]. YouTube. https://youtu.be/5bPzVaxSlQ4

A sample of Kim's short YouTube tips:

Kim Billington- 5. Write a letter to your child: https://youtu.be/g3WvWe_t9QM

Kim Billington- 7. Crying: https://youtu.be/PLzMVvb45C8

Kim Billington- 1. Introduction letter for children: https://youtu.be/guPFgr9D6AE

Kim Billington- 6. Family Meetings: https://youtu.be/HsI_LzYb_9k

Kim Billington- 4. Babushka doll: https://youtu.be/6rC4rH3CcKE

Kim Billington – 10. Therapeutic Story: The Tree at the Crossroads https://youtu.be/0H78nYdwmXA

About the Author

Kim Billington was born in a small village called Disley, in the north of England. Kim wrote her first poem at the age of nine. Three of her poems were published in the *Manchester Evening News* children's pages, and with her postal orders of five shillings each, she bought herself a therapy rabbit, Mr Simply. Together with a teddy bear, Kim survived the challenges of childhood before migrating to Perth, Western Australia with her family when she was 12 years old.

Kim has always had a project on the go: at the age of eight, she was helping neighbours in the village bath their pre-school children and read them bedtime stories. When she was 13, she completed her first sewing masterpiece, a pair of purple bikinis, and at 17, Kim was earning money on the weekends to pay for flying lessons in a small C150. Her career path has also been diverse. She was in the RAAF as an air traffic controller, trained as a teacher, leapt into motherhood and then studied counselling.

Kim has three adult children and is at her happiest in her roles as counsellor, clinical supervisor, workshop facilitator and playful grandma. She loves swimming in the bay near her home in Sandringham, Melbourne.

Kim's current work includes child and family counselling (now often using Zoom online), clinical supervision, supervising Monash University's Masters' of Counselling students, EAP and Carer's counselling.

Methods and tools in Kim's therapeutic toolbox include: mindfulness, narrative therapy, ACT, CFT (Compassion Focused Therapy), creative expressive arts, existential therapy, befriending emotions using metaphors and storytelling, Tree of Life work and creative timelines to understand the life-long emergence of identity.

Kim has previously worked with clients whose adversities include surviving refugee trauma, family violence, divorce, out-of-home care, bereavement, and carers of family members with mental health troubles. She spent three years responding to callers at crisis support services such as 24/7 MensLine, and has also co-facilitated Men's Behaviour Change Groups.

ABOUT THE AUTHOR

Kim's treasure chest of creativity has been overflowing, culminating in writing this book about child counselling, to inspire others who are able to support children and young people on their heroic journeys.

The joy and enthusiasm you will feel when you meet Kim was inherited from her mother, Wyn Billington, who was a psychologist and so much more. Kim's compassion and growth as a counsellor has been born through being with those who bravely share their stories of struggle.

Kim's passion now is sharing creative therapeutic interventions that can bring people renewed hope and understandings about themselves, and fresh ideas about how they want to live in the world.

Kim is available for online family counselling, parent consultations, training, conferences and clinical supervision through:

Website: kimbillington.com.au 'Counselling Conversations'
Email: counsellingconversations@gmail.com.
Instagram: @kim.counselling
Facebook: Kim – Counselling
Qualifications: B. Ed; M. Couns; M. Narrative Therapy & Community Work

About the Illustrator

Tamar Dolev is an award-winning multidisciplinary artist, renowned for her vibrant use of colour. Her practice includes painting, illustration, digital art, sculpture, photography and animation. The colourful and creative world of Tamar stems from her optimistic outlook and how she interprets and gives narratives to the encounters of everyday life.

The surface is a large consideration in her practice, inviting the viewer to engage closely with her work. Collaborating with other artists and continuing to make creative connections is an integral part of Tamar's process.

Tamar holds a fine arts degree from Monash University and has exhibited both Nationally and Internationally.

www.tamardolev.com.au
@theartoftamar
Tamardolev@gmail.com

Acknowledgements

Each person I have met on my journey has shaped who I am. I am grateful to you all. Two people in particular have contributed to my growth as a counsellor.

Firstly, to my mum, Wyn Billington. You were a mature age graduate psychologist in the 1970s. As an 18-year-old I loved sitting by your feet on our balcony overlooking the ocean. Breezes fluttered the many photocopied journals, and the sun warmed the shoeboxes of audio-cassette lecture recordings of Bill O'Hanlon and Frank Farrelly. I was enthralled, and Frank's audacity and deep respect towards his clients has stayed with me.

To dear Dr Ron Findlay. What a phenomenal, and generous narrative therapist. You had a small group of us eager, post-graduate students on the edge of our seats with your wonderful, engaging and dynamic role plays. I entered the lofty world of discussions about post-modern power, and the thrilling ideas of Michel Foucault, Michael White and David Epston. My fondest memories as a graduate student, are of us together on a Friday morning at La Trobe's Bouverie Centre, ready to drink from the deep well of narrative practice.

And significantly, to all the children, adolescents, adults and families who found me in this vast and mysterious cosmos. Thank you for accepting my playful approach to serious problems, and my frank 'strap-on-your-seat-belt' style. From you, I learned more about counselling than any book or course could ever have done. To this day I say to my student counsellors, 'You may be receiving your Masters' degree shortly, but it is your clients who are your professors'.

I acknowledge the Boonwurrung people of the eastern Kulin Nation, on whose unceded lands I live, write and work. I greet my readers today, saying *Wominjeka* which means to come with purpose. I deeply regret that my forefathers from a faraway land, wilfully and shamefully stole land and wages, poisoned, murdered, raped, wrongfully incarcerated, encouraged brutality and chose what some now say is a genocide as a way to ensure ultimate power.

The racism and shocking repercussions of this colonial history continue to this day. It harms each successive generation, in part because the truth has not been told or heard, and is uncomfortable for non indigenous people. My hope is that my small voice will ripple onwards and contribute to changes in awareness and legislation.

My call to action is that we each become a catalyst for change, and for those who are in any position of power, to step up and take responsibility for and make redress for the ongoing devastation in the lives of the original peoples of this beautiful and bountiful land.

Kim Billington

Testimonials

Kim has so many helpful therapeutic activities. I particularly like using the babushka dolls, to symbolise that we all have unmet needs from when we were little. Also, the magical solution book with families, and her use of narrative approaches to 'renew identity, and understand our strengths, to deal with what problems come our way'. Her wonderful practical workshops have motivated me to refresh my narrative practice.
> **Robyn Ball – Circle of Security facilitator**
> **B.Ed; GradDip Infant Mental Health**

Kim has this wonderful manner with children, which immediately lets them know that she's got this, she's got you. She has a vivacious energy and a knowing nature that puts children at ease from the get-go. When you combine this with several years of study honing her craft and back it up with evidence-based modalities, the result is an extremely qualified professional with a winning therapeutic approach, that has helped and supported many children and families along the way.
> **Penny Power – Child & Adolescent Counsellor**
> **BA Coms; M. Couns**

I met Kim a few years ago, when the love of stories brought us together. Our passion built bridges between Brazil and Australia. Exchanges inspired poetry and enchantment. We created together a special narrative story chest. Kim's sensitivity is present in her counselling, where she shares a folktale or short story, inviting the listener to find their own power to illuminate what is most genuine in us. I was happy to hear Kim wanted to include my story about the bird in the cage in this important book.

**Ana Luisa Novis – Clinical Psychologist,
Family Therapist and Author**

Kim helped me grow as a counsellor working with children from a complete beginner. Kim is expressive, creative, resourceful, and full of amazing ideas for counselling activities. She helped me understand the challenges that children and their families face. Kim taught me creative activities and crafts that children and their families love, as well as how to ask questions that can open up therapeutic pathways.

**Linda Yan – Counsellor
B. Psych (Honours). M. Couns**

Kim is an amazing counsellor and supervisor. The knowledge and skills she has passed on to me have been extremely valuable and have changed my approach to counselling, and opened my eyes to the many ways that I can help my clients. I am so grateful for having had the privilege to work with such a knowledgeable and passionate therapist.

**Bianca Brewer – Counsellor
M. Couns; B.Ed**

TESTIMONIALS

As a novice counsellor wanting to work with children, I was able to learn from the workshops on Playful Narrative Therapy by Kim Billington. She shared useful and practical tips and resources, and the art of narrative conversations and mapping the client's journey. I am now able to help clients separate their problems from themselves, explore their values, and provide tailor-made support to meet every client's needs.

Vineeta Giri – Counsellor
M. Couns

Kim has a unique and passionate way of counselling with children. Her use of short stories has helped children deal with whatever issues that they might have. It is hard enough to seek help from as counsellor, let alone talk to a stranger. However Kim has a genuine smile and a calming voice that invites one to feel comfortable.

Fred Wamala
Author; M. Couns; GradCert Men's Violence;
Grad Cert Relationship Counselling

Offers

Purchasing this book is just the beginning. You can access any of these three offers available from Kim's website, Counselling Conversations: www.kimbillington.com.au

1. **SUPERVISION:** For those who require monthly supervision of their clinical practice (through ACA and PACFA), Kim is offering an introductory 30% discount for a first individual session on purchase of this book.

2. **SPEAKER:** Engage Kim to speak at your event. If your group buys 5 copies of Kim's book, she will create a free 60-minute online guest speaker/webinar tailored to your needs. Kim can be booked to be a guest speaker at your university, workplace, radio station, school, parenting group or community hub through the enquiries page on her website. Refer to the speaker bio page for Kim's broad range of topics.

3. **RESOURCES:** Kim has free PDFs of valuable printable tools and resources including the Hero's Journey, Grief and Loss Journey and more available on her website. These tools can be helpful with people of all ages.

Kim Billington

is a dynamic and engaging speaker and trainer in the field of counselling, parenting, topical family issues and facilitating group activities.

Kim has worked with families for over 30yrs, and in the field of family violence, men's behaviour change programs, family separation, bereavement and more. Kim has a Masters' degree in Counselling, B. Ed and a Masters' degree in Narrative Therapy.

Kim initially worked in local government agencies including The City of Melbourne and The City of Port Phillip as a specialist parent support worker. Kim has provided counselling training with The Sydney Centre for Creative Change since 2013, culminating with over 25 online trainings in 2020 during the pandemic lockdown.

Kim's passion is to hear the voice of the child. Even the small voice of our own inner child can benefit from finding a safe space to be heard. Kim believes Children are the Centre of the World.

Kim is a published author of A Counsellor's Companion – creative adventures for child counsellors, parents and teachers.

To enquire about engaging Kim to speak at your next event, email: counsellingconversations@gmail.com for pricings and availabilities, or go to her website: kimbillington.com.au to see her other services, including counselling supervision and free resources.

One example of her popular training is Tree of Life:

This 3 hour creative expressive arts activity can be introduced as a PD or team building experience for professionals in health care, teaching or those wanting to further their personal growth. The tree metaphor is used to express identity evolution through exploring one's past foundations, current strengths, self-care and support networks in the present, and future hopes and dreams.

ACA (Reg: 10222)

PACFA (Reg: 23240)

Notes

NOTES

www.ingramcontent.com/pod-product-compliance
Lightning Source LLC
Chambersburg PA
CBHW071603080526
44588CB00010B/1002